THE CASE AGAINST PORNOGRAPHY

DONALD E. WILDMON

Executive Director, National Federation for Decency

VICTOR BOOKS™

A DIVISION OF SCRIPTURE PRESS PUBLICATIONS INC.
USA CANADA ENGLAND

All Scripture quotations are from the *King James Version*.

Recommended Dewey Decimal Classification: 241.3
Suggested Subject Heading: MORAL THEOLOGY—SINS AND VICES

Library of Congress Catalog Card Number: 86-60853
ISBN: 0-89693-178-1

VICTOR BOOKS,
P.O. Box 1825,
Wheaton, IL 60189.

Contents

This book is dedicated to those individuals who have taken a stand in their local communities against this moral cancer, pornography. Our society is greatly indebted to them. May their numbers increase!

Acknowledgments

Dr. Victor B. Cline, a professor in the Department of Psychology at the University of Utah, is one of the outstanding researchers in the area of pornography, media, and violence. He prepared a paper which he presented to a select group at the University of Utah. That paper appears as the chapter titled "A Psychologist's View of Pornography."

Dr. Elizabeth Holland of Memphis has served as chairman of the Memphis and Shelby County Child Abuse Committee; chairman of pediatrics at St. Joseph Hospital in Memphis; and for the past ten years she has been the doctor at St. Peter's Home for Children in Memphis. She is a graduate of Rhodes University, Memphis, and of the University of Tennessee Medical School. Her remarks are included in the chapter titled "A Pediatrician's View of Pornography."

Dr. Reo Christenson has been professor of political science at Miami University (Oxford, Ohio) since 1956. He is the author of six books and has contributed articles to numerous newspapers, magazines, and professional journals. He is a recipient of both "The Effective Educator Award" voted by Miami University alumni as the professor having the greatest impact on their lives, and the "Benjamin Harrison Award" denoting an educator with a national influence. He has also testified as an expert witness for the prosecution in federal pornography cases. Dr. Christenson gave a presentation at the National Consultation on Pornography, Obscenity, and Indecency. That presentation is included in the chapter titled "A Political Scientist's View of Pornography."

The Rt. Rev. Richard S. Emrich, retired Episcopal bishop of Michigan who now resides in Sun City, Arizona, was among the Christian leaders who spoke out against pornography years ago when it was not necessarily popular to do so. His thoughts are both practical and reasonable. Since mostly Christians will be reading this book, I felt it would be beneficial to include his remarks and have done so in the chapter titled "A Message to the Church."

Publisher's Note

As press time neared for this book, significant changes were taking place in relation to the pornographic plague. Distributors of pornographic magazines were feeling the effects of pressure from those who oppose pornography, especially after the Southland Corporation announced that its 7-Eleven stores would no longer sell *Playboy* and *Penthouse* magazines and other distributors also began to pull offensive magazines. There was a question of how long some of the pornographic magazines could exist without the support of Southland and other big distributors.

By the time you read this book, there could be additional victories to brighten the picture, but you can be sure the battle will be far from over. Many stores will stubbornly continue to peddle filth. And count on those getting richer and richer on pornography to continue to flood the land with various kinds of mind-polluting materials. Thus, this is a much-needed, significant book to give you information on an alarming problem and the know-how in helping put more polluters out of business.

Introduction

There is a great spiritual war being waged. An intentional effort is being made to change the very foundation on which Western civilization is built, to replace the Christian concept of man with a secular and humanist concept.

For the past several years I have racked my brain day after day trying to find some way to get this message across to the Christian community. This is the most frustrating part of my ministry—to get people to listen, to study, to become educated, to open their eyes, to address the problem.

The rank-and-file Christian leader—and even more so the rank and file Christian—has little concept of the fact that we are engaged in a spiritual war. In our so-called mainline denominations (one of which I am a member of), the task of running the denomination and local church is all-consuming. To mention that pornography involves a spiritual war falls on deaf ears. We have a building to build, a budget to raise, a program to continue, an image to protect.

If, a few short years ago, someone had confronted me with the situation from the perspective I now have, I would have turned my back on him, ignored him as being a fanatic or extremist, and gone about my job of running the local church or doing my denominational duty. That is the frustrating part. I know why it is so difficult to reach the rank-and-file Christian leader and, try as I might, I have little success doing it.

All the while the clock keeps ticking, time keeps running out. Within a few short years, without the active involvement of Christian leaders and a host of Christian people, our society will be so saturated with this secular and humanist mindset that the chances of preventing the secular and humanist view of life from becoming the foundation of our society will be nil.

Ignorance and apathy are currently our two deadly sins.

The Christian community is losing this spiritual war. Losing by default. Losing without ever firing a shot. Losing without ever knowing that a war is going on.

What we are up against is not dirty words and dirty pictures. It is a philosophy of life which seeks to remove the influence of Christians and Christianity from our society. Pornography is not the disease but merely a visible symptom. It springs from a moral cancer in our society, and it will lead us to destruction if we are unable to stop it.

Unless the Christian community becomes educated and involved quickly, involvement in as few as five years from now will be meaningless. We will have already lost the war.

Pessimistic? No, realistic.

Weep for our children and grandchildren if we fail.

I only hope that this book helps open minds and hearts and motivates them to involvement.

DONALD E. WILDMON

1.
How Serious Is the Problem?

The phone rang. I answered. It was similar to many calls and letters I receive. This time a mother was calling. She was crying. She wanted help. Her son was deeply involved in pornography and had been for the past two years. She discovered several pornographic magazines such as *Playboy* and *Penthouse* in his room two years ago. He was 15 at that time. She and her husband are devout Christians. Her son, now 17, had been involved in devouring the pornographic magazines. They had tried their best to talk with him. Nothing seemed to work.

I suggested that she seek help from her minister. She said that, strangely, her minister showed no compassion or real concern.

She cried. She apologized for crying. She cried some more. I asked her where her son was getting the magazines. Her reply? From the convenience store nearby. Yet convenience stores have maintained that they sell the filth only to adults. How gullible we have been to believe them! Here was a youth who had been buying the filth since he was 15. Remember how the champions of free speech say that pornography never hurts anyone?

The caller did say that she possibly could get help from the pastor of the Church of the Nazarene in her community. I told her to go to him. You see, the Church of the Nazarene has taken a bold, vocal, and visible stand against pornography and has urged their people to get involved in the battle.

The view of sexuality by this 17-year-old boy has been warped, perhaps for life. There are literally millions of our children and youth who are being told a grand lie about sexuality by pornographers, Hollywood, and the TV networks.

Billy Burden, president of American Renewal Coalition in Dallas, some monthes ago before 7-Eleven pulled pornography, wrote an open letter to the chairman of The Southland Corporation (7-Eleven), urging the chain to stop selling pornographic magazines. Mr. Burden's letter, quoted in part, gives some indication of the impact of pornography on our society:

In 1953 when Hugh Hefner first published *Playboy* magazine, America was not plagued with somebody's wife or daughter being forcibly raped every six minutes. Our small children were not being abducted from our parks and school playgrounds—with many being found later sexually molested and murdered. We were not plagued with 1.5 million missing children. Our teenagers were not conditioned to accept promiscuous lifestyles. We were not plagued with a tidal wave of teenage pregnancy. We were not plagued with an epidemic of venereal diseases like herpes. We were not faced with the ticking time bomb we call AIDS. We were not plagued with a 300% increase in teenage suicide. Today we are! And today pornography is no longer a mere nude in a magazine. Most of the pornography that is being sold today is "sick and perverted!" Could it be, then that pornography is one of the main reasons why America is plagued with the problems I have listed above? The facts reveal, beyond a shadow of a doubt, that it is.

How things have changed since *Playboy* came on the scene in the 1950s!

Pornography. According to *Webster's New Universal Unabridged Dictionary*, it is defined thusly:

1. Originally, a description of prostitutes and their trade.

2. Writings, pictures, etc. intended to arouse sexual desire.
3. The production of such writings, pictures, etc.

However, consider the living definition of pornography. That is what this book is about. Whatever sexual aberration the mind of man can conceive is now available in the area of pornography. Everything from adults having sex with babies just a few months old, to humans having sex with animals, to humans eating the feces of other humans and animals, to humans drinking urine, and on to "snuff" films—where a person is actually killed during the filming of a pornographic movie (having his or her life "snuffed" out)! When we speak of pornography, we aren't talking about bare breasts.

The living definition of pornography includes, among other things, the following:

☐ The FBI estimates that last year in the United States recreational killers murdered 5,000 people. Most of them, say FBI officials, feed on pornography.

☐ According to the FBI, one in four girls who are currently 12 years of age will be sexually assaulted sometime in her lifetime. In other words, 25 percent of girls now entering the teenage years will be sexually assaulted.

Pornographic tapes worth more than $200 million were sold in the Los Angeles area in 1982, and sales since then have continued to soar. According to the California State attorney general's office, video pornographers have close links to organized crime. More profits are made from pornography in the Los Angeles area alone than Sears Roebuck, the leading retailer in America, makes nationwide.

☐ According to former FBI agent Bill Kelly, pornography in America is a $7 billion-a-year industry and growing. And its growth is benefiting primarily organized crime. Kelly says that pornography is invading every part of our lives—even our homes. Kelly was the FBI's top pornography-related crime agent before he retired.

☐ According to columnist Jack Anderson, the Michigan State Police found that pornography is used or imitated in 41 percent of the sex crimes they investigate.

☐ Dr. Victor B. Cline, the University of Utah psychologist whose paper on the effects of pornography appears as chapter 3 in this book, says that the rape rate in the United States has increased by more than 700 percent since 1933. He cites the fact that pornography has been found by many studies to have a direct relationship to these sex crimes.

☐ According to Women Against Pornography, 38 percent of all females in the U.S. will experience some form of sexual abuse before the age of 13. Women Against Pornography estimates that 1.2 million children are annually exploited in commercial sex, such as child prostitution and child pornography. WAP says that of all the reported rapes in this country, half of the victims are under 18 and one-fourth are between 18 and 21; and 50 to 80 percent of all children placed in shelters and juvenile homes, or who otherwise reach the attention of social agencies, have been sexually abused.

☐ Pornography is a dangerous thing, says Roger Miller, retired California lawman. Miller says that whenever he went into the home of a sex crime suspect, he almost *always* found pornography.

☐ According to Senator Christopher Dodd of Connecticut, "By even the most conservative estimates, a child is sexually abused somewhere in this country every two minutes."

☐ NBC News, in a report titled "The Silent Shame," reported that there is "a firm connection between sexual abuse of children and child pornography" and that "the practice of abuse is passed on from one generation to another."
The program also reported:
● A federally funded study in San Francisco found that an estimated one in three girls has been sexually molested. Many experts say the figure for boys might be just as high.
● One sociological study shows that for every case of child

sexual abuse, there are at least nine others we never hear about. Another study shows that the average pedophile, the adult who is attracted to children sexually, molests almost 70 boys and girls.

● United States Postal inspectors have found that 80 percent of the child pornography collectors they investigate abuse children sexually. Chicago police have found an even stronger link between sexual abuse and child pornography. They say that almost all the collectors they investigate convict themselves with their own evidence—Polaroid photographs, videotapes, and movies.

● The U.S. Department of Justice says that child pornography is a 2-3 billion dollar annual business in this country.

☐ Charles H. Keating, founder of Citizens for Decency Through Law, said in testimony before a U.S. Senate hearing that one research study reveals that 77 percent of child molesters of boys and 87 percent of child molesters of girls admitted imitating the sexual behavior they had seen modeled in pornography. Keating also says that since the U.S. relaxed its obscenity laws in the early 1960s reported rapes are up 116 percent and commercialized vice is up by 80 percent.

☐ Human development specialist Dr. Shirley O'Brien of the University of Arizona says that child pornography victimizes as many as 600,000 children in the United States. Victims include children as young as three years old and as old as 18.

Pornography encourages sex crimes, according to detective Joe Smith of the Brocton, Massachusetts Police Department. "See these?" asks Smith, holding up a pile of pornographic magazines. "Every time we search the home of a sex-crime suspect, the house is filled with this stuff!"

Pornographic Magazines, Rape Rate Linked

What two things do the states of Alaska and Nevada have in common? Number one, they lead all other states in readership of pornography per capita. And, number two, they have higher rape rates than all other states. Alaska is number one and Nevada is number two in both categories. These facts appeared in a carefully researched study by Murray Strauss and Larry Baron, sociologists at University of New Hampshire. The study also found, according to its authors, *"an unusually high correlation between sex magazine readership and the rape rate" in different states.*

Data for rape represented only rapes known to and recorded by police, as given in the annual FBI Uniform Crime Reports. Magazines on which the study was based included *Chic, Club, Forum, Gallery, Genesis, Hustler, Oui,* and *Playboy.* Circulation was based on data received from the Audit Bureau of Circulation. With the exception of *Penthouse* (not included because it does not provide circulation data to the ABC), these are by far the most widely read sexually oriented magazines.

Although Strauss stopped short of saying conclusively that reading sex magazines causes rape, the raw data certainly tends to merit that conclusion.

In summarizing the study, Strauss commented: "A Sex Magazine Readership Index . . . was constructed to measure the extent to which mass circulation sex magazines are part of the popular culture of each state. This index was found to be highly correlated with the incidence of rape. Moreover, the significance of this finding is enhanced by: (1) the *contrast with the low correlations of the Sex Magazine Readership with nonviolent crimes;* (2) *the confirmation of the relationships when the analy] sis was replicated for a second year;* and (3) *the persistence of the association despite controls* for possible confounding variables. . . ."

Elsewhere in the study, Strauss stated, "The fact that . . . sex magazine readership . . . is strongly and consistently correlated with rape supports the theory that pornography endorses attitudes that increase the likelihood of rape."

Strauss also commented on laboratory experimental studies which found that exposing men to pornography resulted in increased levels of aggression against women.

"Soft" Pornography Alters Moral Views

Exposure to so-called "soft" pornography (the kind sold by some convenience stores) has greater effects than most people realize. That is the conclusion of Dr. Jennings Bryant, head of the radio-television school of communication at the University of Houston.

Dr. Bryant said, "We're talking about more than sexually violent material. We're finding proof that this (less violent) stuff is doing harm, and something has to be done about it."

Dr. Bryant's study finds that men and women who are exposed to nonviolent pornography have altered views about the roles of family, marriage, and morals in society.

Remember Henry Lee Lucas? From all indications, Lucas is what is known as a "serial killer," an individual who has killed great numbers of people. A Paul Harvey column mentioned him as Harvey dealt with serial killers. Citing the fact that the National Institute of Mental Health is studying the subject, Harvey listed some suspected common denominators among these recreational killers:

● "Most recreational killers are men, are above average in intelligence.

● "An alarming one-out-of-ten are doctors, dentists, or other health professionals.

● "Most, when they are not enraged with sadistic lust appear reassuringly normal, even charming, as they wander the highways and the shopping centers on the prowl for easy victims.

● "The recreational killer rarely knows his victim, according to Dr. Joel Norris, an authority on the subject of serial murders in America.

● "Most killers have cell damage in the brain from abuse or neglect before or after birth. One victim is never enough. The blood lust revives soon and the predator goes hunting again.

● "Most feed on pornography."

In Tulsa, officers searched the home of convicted sex-offender Charles Eric Neal. Buried not far from his home were the bodies of two women. Police said that Neal was connected with the two murders.

Neal had been previously charged in 1983 with sexually assaulting a woman in downtown Tulsa. But the case was dismissed in a preliminary stage.

The nude bodies of the two women were found in graves about four feet deep and 31 feet apart. Police also found in Neal's home magazines depicting sexual bondage.

Sex Killer Ties Pornography to His Serial Murders

"Pornography was not the only negative influence in my life, but its effect on me was devastating," said Arthur Gary Bishop in a statement sent to a recent national conference on pornography. "I would do anything or take any risk to fulfill my deviant desires," he stated.

Bishop, who is on death row for the sex killings of five boys ages 4 to 13, said that if pornography had not been available to him in the early stages of his life, "it is most probable that my sexual activities would not have escalated to the degree they did."

The convicted killer reflected the thinking of University of Utah psychologist Victor Cline, who testified at Bishop's trial that pornography is addictive. "I am a homosexual pedophile convicted of murder," said Bishop, "and pornography was a determining factor in my downfall."

Syndicated Columnist Shocked by Findings

Syndicated columnist Jack Anderson says he has always championed freedom of expression, but his three-month investigation of cable pornography left him stunned.

He says that he found sex orgies that would make the Caesars blush—shows whose producers have the morality of Sodom and Gomorrah.

Anderson points out that our children are getting their sex education from these perverted programs. Usually the children gather at the homes of friends whose parents are out to view such trash.

Many studies give evidence to a statistical relationship between hard-core pornography and sex crimes. Anderson went on to point out that we incarcerate those who commit theft or violence, that we impose quarantines against the spread of communicable diseases. But we do not protect our children from pornography. Anderson joins the ranks of those who acknowledge with alarm how much damage pornography is doing to the children of our society.

Profile of a Rapist

Edna Buchanan, a staff writer for the *Miami Herald*, wrote an article concerning the Pillow Case Rapist, a person who committed a number of rapes in her area. Scientists at the FBI Academy in Quantico, Virginia, at the request of Metro police, studied the rapes and prepared a five-page psychological profile of the rapist. Among the characteristics which the scientists listed for the rapist was this one: "He collected *Playboy*, then *Penthouse* magazines . . . and dreamed of rape. Then he slipped over the threshold of fantasy into the reality of sexual assault."

But still those who produce and sell pornography tell us that their publications and movies do not cause people to commit the acts they see. They say that magazines such as *Playboy* and *Penthouse* are harmless.

In another study, the FBI's most ambitious attempt to create a profile of a sex killer, found that such men who kill—and kill again—often cannot tell the difference between reality and fantasy, even when they are committing murder.

FBI interviews with 36 convicted sex killers—including many serial murderers—reveal that virtually all of them have long-standing fantasies of murder that are "as real to them as their acts of murder."

The FBI report said that the 36 killers were usually Caucasian and eldest sons who grew up in homes where alcohol abuse was a big problem. Most of the offenders "did not have a satisfactory relationship with their fathers." In addition, the report said that 81 percent of the sex killers reported their biggest sexual interest was in reading pornographic materials and in compulsive masturbation.

The coast-to-coast interviews with the jailed killers, who were not identified, were part of an FBI effort to develop a psychological profile of sex murderers in an effort to track down future killers faster.

Pornography Not Just a Money-making Business

Dr. Charles Stanley, speaking as president of the Southern Baptist Convention, stated: "Pornography is not just a money-making business. It is a very shrewd, effective way to destroy this country. History reveals that nations who have given themselves over to sensuality have been destroyed. Pornography, sensuality, lesbianism, and homosexuality divide the mind and dull the consciences of men and women. If we keep pushing drugs, sex, and pornography, we will absolutely anesthetize ourselves into oblivion."

"Many people do not realize the emotional and psychological dangers to children and teenagers coming from sexually explicit films," says Kenneth Kelzer, a California clinical social worker.

In a letter to the editor of his hometown paper, Kelzer called cable television's new wave of pornographic movies a form of air pollution. Kelzer wrote: "It is quite possible for children to be overstimulated sexually and suffer harmful effects from (these pornographic films) later in their adult years. Highly charged erotic films . . . become destructive when viewed by younger people."

Statistics bear out these comments. Sex offenders now outnumber any other category of inmates in Minnesota prisons. Sex offenders make up a whopping 18.5 percent of the total population in Minnesota, eclipsing armed robbers. Of 2,323 prison inmates, a total of 430 were behind bars for rape and other sex crimes.

Kelzer also attacks the cry from pornography pushers that parents should control their children's viewing. It is obvious, said Kelzer, that parents cannot be all places at all times. The social worker contends that the wisest and most practical place to draw the line on pornography is to keep it off the air waves entirely.

Policeman Tells Terrors Caused by Pornography

"I believe pornography does lead to other crimes," says Roger Miller, retired veteran of law enforcement in Kansas and California.

On vice patrol in Wichita, Miller says that he "investigated just about every kind of crime or criminal act that can be committed." Whenever he went into the home of a sex crime suspect, he almost *always* found pornography. Pornography, according to Miller, is a dangerous thing—just as dangerous as drugs and alcohol. In fact, Miller says pornography can be *more* dangerous than alcohol and drugs. Most often, the person using drugs and alcohol ends up being the only victim. But pornography starts the reader looking for a victim other than himself.

Bob Coffman, at one time a pornography addict, has more recently been part of a successful drive to clean up smut in his hometown and in four neighboring towns. Coffman's interest in removing pornography from the family marketplace is intense because he knows the damage pornography can do to an individual.

He says pornography encourages one to consider a lot of perverted practices that would not be involved in a healthy relationship between man and wife. His belief is backed up by many marriage counselors who point out that pornography is frequently involved with couples coming for counseling.

Coffman says, "As a child who was involved, almost totally involved, in lustful sex through pornography, I can say that you are not able to concentrate on learning to read or anything else. Your mind is full of sex. Reports show that 75 to 90 percent of the pornography that is bought ends up in the hands of kids."

Why Fight Pornography?

"I'd rather have a child crippled by polio than crippled by early involvement in sex," says Beverly Hills psychiatrist Melvin Anchell.

Strong words—and an attitude many of us might think cruel and insensitive. But consider the fact that in his years as medical doctor and psychiatrist, Anchell has treated many children damaged by smut and pornography. He believes that pornographic shows and movies disturb, rather than enhance, normal sex growth, family life, and morality.

In his book, *Sex and Insanity,* Dr. Anchell says that pornography affects children just as a child molester does. It causes emotional damage that may never be repaired.

In the same book, he tells of a 17-year-old boy who came to be treated for headaches. Anchell quickly found the real problem was pornography. The boy and friends started at age 12 to view sex films owned by the parents. They imitated what they saw, then created their own perversions. At age 15, the boy could perform only when under the influence of drugs. At 17, he satisfied his perversion by beating his nude partners.

So devastating is pornography that Surgeon General C. Everett Koop, declaring that the country is at a moral crossroads, announced a major offensive against violence and pornography in American society. He told a meeting of Christian leaders in Washington, D.C. that the cheapening of human life and deteriorating moral standards could set off a wave of social chaos and brutality in the next several decades.

Dr. Koop said: "If you don't believe me, watch one of the television stations that shows video rock in the afternoon and see the senseless crossroads of violence with the senseless pornography of this age, but all to the beat of the music that our young poeple have made part of their lives."

President's Commission Impartial?

Remember the 1970 President's Commission on Pornography and Obscenity? Strangely, that group wanted pornography made legal and issued a recommendation for the repeal of all pornography and obscenity laws. Edward E. Elson, chairman of the Atlanta News Agency, was a member of that group. The Atlanta News Agency isn't known for carefully screening magazines it distributes. For example, the agency is one of the largest distributors of *Penthouse*. It seems logical that the owner of such an agency would want laws that would favor his business, doesn't it?

Even federal funds have been used to help the enemy. Women for Pornography sponsored a pornographic art show with tax dollars. The exhibit portrayed almost every imaginable perverted sex practice in a New York gallery. More than $200 thousand tax dollars had been channeled into the host gallery through recent grants from the National Endowment for the Arts, a government agency operating on more than $166 million in taxpayer funds.

The Women for Pornography show was described by the participants as "an erotic and pornographic carnival." It was called "Carnival Knowledge, Second Coming," and it included sculpture, photography, and crude drawings depicting both homosexual and heterosexual acts, many in sado-masochist situations. Press releases on the "Carnival" display came complete with photos of topless feminists who used the taxpaper dollars in their exhibition to talk about oral sex, among other things. Also the exhibit included photos of nude children.

According to the *New York Times*, other recent grants to the gallery include the following: $73,000 from New York State Council on the Arts and unspecified amounts from Exxon Corporation, Mobil Foundation, and F.W. Woolworth Company.

Pornography pays handsome profits to distributors. Those who oppose this filth in the marketplace are often the object of retaliation. A University of Wisconsin-Madison student lost her job at a campus store for refusing to sell *Playboy*, *Penthouse*, and *Playgirl* magazines. Mary Process told the campus paper that the management of the Union South student center asked her to resign because she refused to sell the magazines during her shift.

"I think it's a real injustice to force women to sell them. Why should I have to sell this to someone who someday might rape me or some other woman?" Miss Process said.

All aspects of pornography are damaging, according to a recent study by David Scott, a psychotherapist from Toronto. The report says so-called "soft core" pornography breeds sexual dissatisfaction and helps break up marriages. All who view pornography, even for short periods of time, are affected by it.

Built on the mass consumption of "soft core" materials is an addictive pyramid of increasingly bizarre and violent activities, culminating in rape, child abuse, and sex murders, according to a report published by the Child and Family Protection Institute in Washington.

Silence Lends Acceptance

Our silence to the onslaught of pornography has tended to say that we accept it. This is the conclusion of John Court in his book *Pornography: A Christian Critique.* "In many places, the availability of pornography depends on the assumption that community standards have changed so that sensible citizens now accept its presence. There is really no evidence to sustain that position, but so long as responsible citizens remain silent, certainly the *appearance* of change is there. So long as the aggressive minority shout for removal of restrictions and the voice of decency remains muted, the politicians and legislators may be forgiven for believing there has been a change," Court wrote.

Also, most of us would rather not be deluged with a shower of information concerning pornography. But if we are to see progress in the battle against pornography, we must continue to remind ourselves of some of the basics—both in the area of why the public remains silent, and in the area of the devastating effects pornography has on people's lives.

I received a copy of an article from the Bellevue, Washington *Journal American* which addressed both areas briefly, but effectively. The article says the public has not demanded action on the pornography issue for several reasons:

Lack of information on how degrading and violent pornography has become. Today's magazines, films, and videotapes, it was pointed out, include promiscuity, bestiality, rape, and "snuff" films which show actual murders, plus about anything else the deviate human mind can dream up.

Ignorance of the harmful effects pornography has on society. After one's mind feeds on that kind of material over a period of time, it becomes part of the person and will eventually translate into behavior in one form or another.

Fear of being labeled a censor or book burner. The fact is that obscenity laws are not censorship. Laws of various types are necessary for our protection and well-being.

The belief that pornography is protected under the First

Amendment free speech rights. Actually, the Supreme Court has said that obscene material is not protected by the First Amendment.

Sex crimes will continue to increase in number as long as decent Americans remain silent. It is time for all of us to stand up and speak out, and to call pornography what it really is—a devastating cancer pushed by people whose only interest is making a fast dollar.

Dr. James Draper, past president of the Southern Baptist Convention and a friend of mine, said that decency is "something that's basic to all of us, whether we be Protestant, Catholic, or Jew.

"We all share a basic commitment to decency, a basic commitment to morality . . . and we all believe in the holiness of God," Draper said. "Pornography—in movies, on television, and on the printed page—is something we've been silent about too long. We have been content to do our thing and let the world fall apart."

Draper urged people to work together on this problem. "Anytime Christians can get together on something, we can be salt and light (to society) and everything God has said we're supposed to be."

Robert P. Dugan, director of the Office of Public Affairs for the National Association of Evangelicals, wrote: "That sex crimes are on the increase should not surprise us. As long as our society, including evangelical Christians, is willing to tolerate pornography, the incidence of rape, child molestation, and sex abuse will grow."

Some Are Taking Action
A few have been working, against all odds, to combat pornography. One such person is Father Bruce Ritter. Those who argue that pornography is harmless should talk with Father Ritter, director of Covenant House in New York City's Times Square district. Each year, Father Ritter helps some 12,000 young people under 21—homeless, runaway, and hungry kids who

come to Times Square in search of money or excitement and who end up the prey of pimps and pornographers.

He says that fully 60 percent of those he helps have been involved in prostitution or pornography. Father Ritter wishes he could talk with anyone who thinks pornography is a "victimless" crime and to those who, by their silence, allow the pornography industry to flourish. He would tell them story after story of children who are shot full of drugs by their pimps, bought and sold like merchandise, tortured, imprisoned, and, yes, even killed.

Father Ritter would tell them about the 14-year-old boy who was chased into Covenant House by a pimp waving a broken bottle. The boy had just escaped from the motel up the street where he had been held prisoner for six weeks.

Father Ritter would tell about the ten-year-old boy who arrived carrying the toy cars his customers gave him as payment.

He would tell them about 11-year-old Veronica, arrested eight times for prostitution. Each time her pimp paid her $100 fine and put her back on the street. Shortly after her twelfth birthday, Veronica was thrown to her death from a tenth-story window by either her pimp or a customer.

What draws a young person into prostitution or pornography in the first place? Father Ritter says it is simple—children are seducible. They are seduced by words, by gifts, by money, by actions, by pictures. Many—the runaways and the homeless—are also driven by the need to survive.

He also points out that it is tragic that we talk of moral outrage when children are being bought and sold and we do nothing about it. It is tragic when we wring our hands over the suffering, hurt, and pain inflicted upon innocent young children by the pimps and prostitutes, yet remain silent when we buy products from the local convenience stores which stock and sell pornographic magazines.

Father Ritter concludes that we are a society with no fortitude, afraid to take moral positions, afraid to lose friends. Thus this evil thing—pornography and the whole illegal sex industry—continues to flourish.

Our silence has caused many people to confuse lust with love. A former striptease dancer says in her book *Naked Is the Best Disguise: My Life as a Stripper* (Morrow, 1984), that she was seeking admiration she believed she could get from strangers in seedy bars. Lauri Lewin, a 24-year-old college graduate, says she now recognizes that she was seeking a kind of acceptance and attention lacking at home.

She was three when her parents divorced, and lived with her mother until she was 14. At that time she moved to Boston to live with her father. At 16, she began her career as a stripper in Boston's Combat Zone, a few blocks of strip bars, peep shows, and pornographic shops. (At 16 she began stripping. And the pornographers always tell us that they don't allow minors to view or participate in their filth!)

She also developed a $100-a-day cocaine habit. Pornography, you see, is closely tied in with drugs. Miss Lewin says she saw stripping as a glamorous make-believe world, that it seemed like show business. She required six months of therapy to leave the sordid life behind. And still we are told that pornography doesn't harm anyone.

Does Anyone Preach Against Pornography?

My friend Bill Kelly, the retired FBI officer previously quoted in connection with his enforcement of pornography and obscenity statutes, reports that during a recent trial the judge asked three questions of persons in the courtroom. First, "Have you, or has anyone in your family, been a victim of sexual abuse?" In response about 10 percent of the hands went up. The second question was, "Have you ever read or even paged through a pornographic magazine?" About 40 percent of the hands went up. Question three was, "Have you *ever* heard a sermon preached on pornography or obscenity?" Not a single hand was raised.

This highlights the problem. Most church people are not aware of what pornographic magazines are showing—publications that are having a tremendous influence, polluting countless minds. There are enough of them printed every year (240 million!) to pave a two-lane highway with their covers, from San Francisco to Washington, D.C. And the church has barely raised its voice.

"The church must determine to break out of its silence," said Dr. Paul Tanner, executive secretary of the Church of God, Anderson, Indiana. "We must stop losing this battle by default," he said.

Tanner went on to say, "If Christians do not defend Christian morality, who will? It is past time. We must not be intimidated by those who charge us with prudishness or latter-day puritanism. The 'Playboy philosophy' of sexually using and discarding another person with 'no strings attached' is not a form of freedom but of enslavement.

"This porno-plague will not die of its own shallowness. Pornography is an insatiable cancer: it stalks and devours, with ever-increasing appetite.

"Hugh Hefner and Larry Flynt act as though they invented sex. Their kinky counsel that glamorizes incest, adultery, bestiality, and homosexuality is as old as the mummies of Egypt. Read Leviticus and you will see that 15 centuries ago God destroyed whole nations for what these perverted minds think is so modern."

Dr. Tanner's remarks should be heeded. Sometimes, however, they will fall on deaf ears. A pastor recently wrote me a most interesting letter. It could have been written by many pastors. The letter began: "Our congregation, as such, does not involve itself in social, political, or parachurch processes." I wonder what the congregation does involve itself in? Church suppers? Annual bazaars? Committee meetings? The church which does not involve itself in anything other than preaching, praying, and eating should really not call itself a church, but rather a social club.

Pornographers are not just satisfied with pornography; they are also pushing a philosophy of life—a worldview. And, because it is at odds with the Christian philosophy, they feel they must destroy the Christian philosophy. They do this not only with their pornographic pictures and wording but in other ways. One example of this is *Hustler*, the pornographic magazine owned by

Larry Flynt. At the top of the credits page in the anti-Christian pornographic magazine Flynt lists "Jesus H. Christ, Esq." as publisher and Larry Flynt as editor! The magazine is filled with sick cartoons belittling and demeaning Christians and Christianity.

Doing Good the Wrong Way

Here's one for the books. In Millbrae, California the local Muscular Dystrophy Association sold tickets for $4 each to raise funds. The tickets offered men a chance to win a date with a pair of *Penthouse* centerfold girls. It is sad when a community offers an opportunity for its citizens to win a date with pornography stars. Doing wrong things for right reasons is a sure way to destruction. The drive to raise funds to fight muscular dystrophy by using pornography stars is indicative of how much some leaders in our society have adopted the humanistic, anti-Christian philosophy.

William Buckley wrote recently that the permissiveness of which modern liberals are so proud produces results we *all* deplore. Buckley goes on to point out that in the past 20 years pornographic literature has invaded our society at all levels, information about birth control has become readily available to all, the pill has been proclaimed the great emancipator of women, and homosexuals have been given the stamp of approval by the liberals.

What is the result of these so-called liberal advancements in our society? Pornography and sex crimes have skyrocketed. We have given forth more birth control information than any society in history, and illegitimacy is higher than it has ever been. The practice of homosexuality is more widely accepted than ever in our society, and we now have AIDS.

Buckley went on to point out the correlation between illegitimate births and poverty, and concluded that sexual permissiveness has caused a rise in disease and a rise in illegitimacy and illegitimacy has caused a rise in poverty. The results of the liberal, secular, humanist approach to life is reduced morals, betrayed children, disease, and poverty.

Buckley's conclusion was no surprise. The results were predictable. Those who scorn and reject Christian values must eventually pay the price of doing so—in this world as well as in the world to come.

Two decades ago, physicians knew of five venereal infections. Now there are at least 20 diseases transmitted through sexual contact. Sexually transmitted diseases will cost the nation up to $3 billion this year. And this monetary cost is minor when compared to the devastating physical and emotional effects on individuals.

Both sexes suffer, but women are harder hit. Many of the sexually transmitted diseases also cause harm to infants born to the mothers with these infections.

Chicago Tribune columnist Joan Beck warns women who live high-risk lifestyles that they may have to suffer the consequences. In other words, promiscuity and a free-wheeling sexual lifestyle may well exact a painful price.

Charles H. Keating, Jr., of Citizens for Decency Through Law, once wrote:

I've been leading the fight against pornography in this country since 1957. But pornography has now become so unimaginably worse that only the most insanely perverse minds could have conceived it. It goes beyond obscenity, beyond masochism, beyond child pornography as we know it.

It is this. There has begun in this country a nationwide campaign to normalize sex between adults and *young children*—to promote incest. This is where the pornographers have finally led us. This is where we find ourselves, a nation being taught to devour its own children to satisfy a sexual appetite as monstrous as anything Satan himself could conceive.

The signs are everywhere.

The otherwise naked *Playboy* centerfold wears bobby sox and saddle shoes and a little-girl ribbon in her hair. Men's magazines are filled with stories of loving daddies who initiate their daughters into the "beauty of father-daughter sex." So-called sex psychologists write newspaper columns describing the "benefits" of incest, calling it the "last taboo," as though it were some primitive and uncivilized belief.

If this is allowed to go any further, does anyone doubt that God should destroy us? For the sake of our sanity, for the sake of our children, we must stop this insane trend before it goes further.

Unless we can blunt this deadly trend . . . nothing else of value will remain in our beloved country. Childhood innocence, family love, decency, morality—all will be dead. And somewhere, someplace, a pillar of salt will mark a nation that sacrificed its very own children upon the devil's altar of sexual obsession.

How serious is the problem? Edward Gibbon in his *Decline and Fall of the Roman Empire* said that the following five attributes marked Rome at its end:
- a mounting love of show and luxury;
- a widening gap between the very rich and the very poor;
- an obsession with sex;
- freakishness in the arts, masquerading as originality, and enthusiasms pretending to be creativity;
- an increased desire to live off the state.

America and Rome. We are beginning to have a lot in common.

2.
Pornography in the Family Marketplace

Through the years the general public has associated pornography with sleazy bookstores and theaters. However, in the '70s and '80s many of the major players in the game of pornography are well-known household names. For example, 7-Eleven convenience stores were for a lengthy period the leading retailers of pornographic magazines in America.

Indeed, 7-Eleven was perhaps the most important key to successful marketing of pornography in the family marketplace. That, of course, changed in April 1986 when the Southland Corporation, parent firm of 7-Eleven, announced that it was pulling pornography. Southland recognized that violence is apparently associated with pornographic magazines and therefore these publications were out of place in stores serving families, according to the announcement that brought applause across the country. This was indeed a bold move and Southland is to be commended for the action, for profits made by 7-Eleven on pornography ran into the millions of dollars. In a court hearing in 1984, Erwin Billman, then executive vice president of *Penthouse* magazine, testified that Southland Corporation was the single most important outlet for the sales of *Penthouse* (U.S. District Court, Northern District of Georgia—Civil Action C77-1238A). 7-Eleven sold more *Playboy* magazines through its stores than any other retailer in America (*Everybody's Business-An Almanac*, Harper & Row, 1980).

Time, Inc. has moved into the sex film market with offerings on their Cinemax cable television channel. Time is offering many of the same movies which are on the Playboy Channel service—titles such as *Naughty Wives*, *Young Lady Chatterly*, *Hollywood Hot Tubs*, *New York Nights*, *Intimate Moments*, etc.

SpectraVision, headquartered in Richardson, Texas, offers a sex film service which can be found in many hotels and motels.

Other companies involved in the pornography business include the distributors of pornographic magazines. Some of the major ones are:

● Kable News Company (owned by AMREP Corporation, chairman Howard W. Friedman), 777 Third Avenue, New York; distributes *Club*, *Club International*, *Family Affairs*, *Fox Magazine*, *Gallery*, *High Society*, *Live*, *Letters*, and *Pocketfox*.

● Curtis Circulation Company (a division of Cadence Industries, chairman Sheldon Feinberg, which also owns Marvel Comic Group), 841 Chestnut, Philadelphia; distributes *Forum*, *Penthouse*, *Genesis*, *Swank*, *Velvet*, *Variations*, *Penthouse Letters*, and *Girls of Penthouse*.

● Warner Publisher Services (a division of Warner Communications, chairman Steven J. Ross, which also owns Cosmos Soccer Club, Franklin Mint, Warner Brothers, Panavision, and DC Comics), 666 Fifth Avenue, New York; distributes *Cheri*, *Playboy*, *Oui*, *Playboy Specials*, and *Playgirl*.

The information above comes from the December 1984 edition of *Magazine and Bookseller*. More than 400 wholesale agencies across the nation perform the task of getting the publications delivered, stocked, and displayed in stores.

Importance of News Outlets

Pornographic magazines rely heavily for their circulation on single-issue or over-the-counter sales in addition to subscriptions. Therefore their display at newsstands and in stores is vital to their existence. In fact, the subscription market of *Penthouse* magazine *amounts to only about 5 percent of total sales*. Only 202,877 individuals subscribed to *Penthouse* magazine during the last half of 1984, but an average of 3,568,517 were purchased monthly over the counter. (*Report on the Multi-Billion Dollar Traffic in Pornography*, prepared by Morality in Media, and testimony by Erwin Billman—Northern District of Georgia, Civil Action C77-1238A.)

Pornography for Cash

One of the favorite arguments of pornographers and stores which sell pornographic magazines is that they don't sell to minors. But consider this excerpt from a letter from a man in Friendswood, Texas:

"Back in June or July I got mad about pornography—especially after sending an 11-year-old into a Stop & Go store, where she bought a copy of *Genesis* without a question. An 11-year-old girl bought a pornographic magazine and no questions were asked. And we are told that the pornographic magazines aren't sold to children."

An isolated case, you say? The letter continues. "Also a very young looking 15-year-old bought *Playboy* and *Oui* without a question." Not quite as isolated as pornography people want you to believe.

A Muskegon, Michigan mother recently wrote me with her concerns about material her 15-year-old daughter had received in the mail. She sent me a package which her daughter had received from *Playgirl* magazine urging her daughter to subscribe. *Playgirl* is the pornographic magazine read by some females and also by male homosexuals. The mother was understandably upset.

"My 13-year-old son purchased and brought home what he thought was a monster comic book," wrote Mrs. Cyndy Horn in the Fairfield, California *Daily Republic*. "He had only looked at the cover when it was purchased. We both were shocked when looking through it—the pornographic pictures and language were shocking." The disturbed mother reported that they returned to the store and were again shocked to see pornography intermingled with regular comic books. The cashier refunded her son's money, but was not concerned about promoting pornography among children.

The following editorial appeared in the *Orem-Geneva Times* published in Orem, Utah. The writer reflected on the infamous Utah case resulting in the conviction of Arthur Gary Bishop for sexual abuse and murder of young boys.

To sentence a man to death once the crime is committed is merely putting a finger in the dike. There'll be another time, another place, another victim, and another [Arthur Gary] Bishop . . . and another . . . and another.

The fuel that fires such crimes is pornography. A society that expresses shock and horror at crimes of rape, murder, child abuse, yet allows pornography in all its guises to spread its foul poison upon the witting and unwitting alike, is guilty, at least, of aiding and abetting.

Soft porn has invaded television, movies, newspapers, books, and family magazines. What once was abhorrent has become acceptable. Hard porn is creeping in—movie ratings are no longer reliable as public opinion yields to repetition.

The facts are that pornography first contaminates, then cripples, then kills. Great nations have fallen as societies are weakened by this sickness.

Pornography Connected to Crime

The fact that pornography contaminates, cripples, and kills is easily identified by those dealing with the problem. Sergeant Dave Wright of the Brockton, Massachusetts Police Department says he gets a rape report on his desk an average of every other day, and he believes television is partially responsible.

Wright cites the recent example of a 12-year-old boy who attacked a young girl after he got the idea from television.

The police sergeant goes on to say he feels society is sick. When asked what caused this, he said, "The lack of religion, the breakdown of the family, the breakdown of schools, the lack of morals. Nothing is taboo anymore.''

Wright's colleague, Detective Joe Smith, had some words about pornographic magazines.

"See these," said Smith, holding up a pile of pornographic magazines, "every time we search the home of a sex-crime suspect, the house is filled with this stuff.''

Deputy Prosecutor Phil Blowers of Indianapolis asks: "Why do we teach our young people with books and pictures if this material doesn't make impressions upon their minds and educate them to action?''

In addition to the convenience, drug, and other "family" type stores, the military exchanges are major distributors of pornography. The U.S. government fosters and encourages pornography which is aimed at the primarily young male market of the U.S. armed services. The National Federation for Decency has received numerous complaints about the distribution of pornography through military exchange systems.

Hotel gift shops and airport magazine racks are also primary sources for pornography.

Video Cassette Industry

As the popularity of the video cassette recorder has increased, the marketing of pornographic video cassettes has become a multimillion dollar industry. Major suppliers of hardcore X-rated video cassettes reported sales increases in 1984 that ranged 30-50 percent above 1983 with expectations that the growth rate will continue. Video cassettes are marketed through video stores, department stores, supermarkets, convenience stores, and other outlets.

Today there is at least one VCR in each of 20 million homes— about one in five of the nation's television households. National Video, one of the nation's largest video retail chains, has 520 stores nationwide. It is estimated that there are more than 14,000 "mom-and-pop" video stores of which approximately 75 percent carry pornographic video cassettes.

One of the largest drugstore chains in America now sells and rents X-rated video cassettes. In one promotional piece, the stores offered pornography at about 10-20 percent lower than the regular pornographic bookstores. At least ten movies in the drug chain's video cassette catalog specialize in rape, gang bang, sadomasochism and/or bondage.

The chain offers approximately 250 X-rated movies such as *Daddy's Little Girls, Ball Game, Blow Hard, Bodies in Heat, Centerspread Girls, Inside Seka,* and *Nasty Nurses.* Other titles include: *School Girls, Desires Within Young Girls, French School Girls, Private School Girls,* and *The Younger the Better.*

Liberal Media and ACLU Help Pollute

Of course, the acceptance of pornography in the family marketplace could not have occurred without the tacit approval by the liberal media of *Playboy* and similar magazines and the philosophy behind them. Of course, pornography has always existed, but it has not enjoyed the acceptance of the media elite and at times the protection of the courts that it now enjoys. In days gone by pornography was treated and handled as contraband. But the approval of pornography by many in the media, and the defense afforded it by the American Civil Liberties Union, has made it an acceptable item in otherwise "family" stores. Their approval made *Playboy, Penthouse,* and similar magazines acceptable and opened the door for the imitators. The spread of pornography has also been aided and abetted, under the guise of protecting the First Amendment, by such organizations as the American Civil Liberties Union. So strong has been the support of pornography by the ACLU that the organization criticized a new study on pornography even before the study began! Concerning the attorney general's Commission on Pornography, Barry Lynn, ACLU legislative counsel, said a major national discussion that "begins with the erroneous assumption that explicit sexual speech is a major national problem . . . poses great, great dangers to the First Amendment."

Assistant Attorney General Mit Spears, who heads the Office of Legal Policy at the Justice Department, said he found Lynn's views "an incredible statement. If there's anyone coming into this with a closed mind, I think he's demonstrated where he's coming from.''

It is striking that the ACLU, which consistently says it opposes censorship, wanted to censor a study on pornography!

Despite the ACLU cries that pornography is protected by the First Amendment, Supreme Court Chief Justice Warren Burger wrote:

> To equate the free and robust exchange of ideas and political debate with commercial exploitation of obscene material demeans the grand conception of the First Amendment and its high purposes in the historic struggle for freedom. The protection given speech and press was fashioned to assure unfettered interchange of ideas for the bringing about of political and social changes desired by the people. But the public portrayal of hard-core sexual conduct for its own sake, and for the ensuing commercial gain, is a different matter.

This interest in protecting the producers of pornography by the ACLU may be a surprise to some, but it isn't to those who know the connection. The bond between the Playboy Foundation and the American Civil Liberties Union is strong. Pornography is the common cause that binds them so closely together: Playboy peddles it; ACLU defends it.

ACLU Impartial?

For years many have been misled to view the ACLU as an impartial guardian of the First Amendment. Meanwhile, the ACLU has built a reputation for defending pornographers, contending that regulation or restriction of pornography traffic would constitute infringement of First Amendment rights. Because of the ACLU's defense of pornography, the Playboy Foundation helps the ACLU in many ways.

This was indicated in "The Bunny Is Serious," an article in the September 1984 *American Bar Association Journal*. Carol Pitchersky, associate director of the ACLU, states, "We have a very good working relationship with the Playboy Foundation.

Not only does it contribute money, but foundation leaders are involved in the organization in other important ways.

"Christie Hefner, for example, sits on the boards of two of our state affiliates and is a member of an important leadership group of the national ACLU." Miss Hefner, daughter of *Playboy* magazine founder Hugh Hefner, currently heads the Playboy sex empire.

Burton Joseph, Playboy Foundation's executive director, is also a Chicago civil liberties lawyer.

The Playboy Foundation was created in 1969 after Bill Helmer, senior editor of *Playboy* magazine, came on staff. In the *Journal* article, Helmer states, "We were constantly getting letters from people distressed and in trouble with the law. Many were having trouble with drugs, sex laws, kids busted for marijuana, somebody busted for consensual oral sex in Wisconsin.

"Initially, *Playboy* was taking an editorial stand, quarreling with the existence of those laws. The Playboy Foundation was created to challenge those laws and assist other organizations, like the ACLU, in challenging those laws."

Playboy and the ACLU complement each other well in their common goal—one producing pornography, the other protecting it. The ACLU, like *Playboy*, clearly wants to keep pornography in the family marketplace.

One should not think that the pornographers aren't interested in politics, either. The Playboy Foundation awarded its 1984 Hugh M. Hefner First Amendment Award to Frank Wilkinson. Wilkinson is a longtime identified member of the Communist Party USA. The $3,000 cash prize was, of course, made possible by those who advertise in and purchase *Playboy* magazine.

A recent issue of *Human Events* reported that Playboy Enterprises has contributed funds to the proabortion group Catholics for a Free Choice, organized to oppose the Catholic Church's stand against abortion. When asked why she accepts grants from Playboy Enterprises, Frances Kissling, executive director of Catholics for a Free Choice, insisted, "I've never felt that by taking money from someone indicates that we support them." The criterion to determine whether or not to accept money is whether that source would interfere with the abortion group's goals. She went on to say that *Playboy* has never interfered with their goals.

Interestingly, she was quoted in 1983 as saying that her group would never accept grants from *Hustler* magazine because "there are boundaries of good taste." *Playboy* money is OK, but *Hustler* money is dirty. Didn't Jesus say something about swallowing a camel and strangling on a gnat?

Are the other pornographic magazines any different in philosophy from *Playboy?* According to Dorchen Leidholdt of Women Against Pornography, any distinction between *Playboy* magazine and *Hustler* magazine is false and misleading.

No Difference in Message

"The message of *Playboy,*" says Miss Leidholdt, "is essentially the same as the message of *Hustler,* and that is: Women are nothing more than sexual commodities to be bought and sold, used and discarded."

Playboy is more insidious than other pornographic publications in Miss Leidholdt's view, because it's slick and includes articles which supposedly justify its existence.

Miss Leidholdt also observes that it is hypocritical for *Playboy* to provide money for feminist groups and causes and, at the same time, engage in sexual exploitation through *Playboy* magazine. The Playboy Foundation is a large contributor to the National Organization for Women and gives thousands of dollars in free advertising to Norman Lear's organization People for the American Way. One can conclude that Lear and his group think that pornography is the American way.

And yet, many people would have us believe that *Playboy* and other expressions of pornography, from which many "respectable" companies have profited, has had a liberating effect on our society, bringing about more openness and freedom. *Playboy,* they argue, never harmed anyone. Yet nothing could be farther from the truth. I'm sure you have heard the cliché arguments that pornography is a victimless crime and that no girl has ever been harmed by a book. You will find much in these pages to refute those theories of the liberal intellectuals, but consider the following story from a woman in one of our Western states:

DEAR MR. WILDMON:

I am sending you my story in hopes that it will help convince some people that *Playboy* is addictive and it harms innocent people. Please do not use my name.

First, I will give some background information. I am a middle child of a family of five. We were and still are a very religious family.

When I was 12 years old, my older brother, who was then nearly 16, got hooked on *Playboy*. My brother's bedroom was in the basement in our home, and my mother would have me go down to my brother's bedroom and call him for dinner, or whatever. On several occasions I would "catch" my brother looking at *Playboy* when he was "studying for school." He would quickly hide the magazine when I opened his door. When he came home from school, he would go down to his bedroom to study, and would shut his door. I always knew that he would be looking at his *Playboy* magazines. When my brother wasn't at home, I would go into his room and look where my brother had hidden his magazines. I would always hope that they wouldn't be there. The thoughts of them there made me feel sick inside. I knew it was wrong, and he knew it too. But I told no one about them.

One day when we were having a get-together at our home, I was sent downstairs to get my brother and cousin. They were in the recreation room. They didn't hear me coming, and when I walked into the room I saw that my cousin was masturbating with my brother looking on. Back then I had no idea what masturbating was, but I do now. I felt sick. I never told anyone because I was scared and embarrassed. I knew that the *Playboy* magazines they looked at had much to do with "their filthy minds."

As time went on I noticed that my brother became obsessed with females. He told dirty jokes with his friends, and listened to filthy tape recordings when no one was around the house but me. I was very naive, but I knew that what he was doing was wrong.

One day my mother sent me to the basement to get something from the storage room for her. I had to go through a dark, small hallway to get to our storage room. When I was in the hallway, my older brother reached out from behind me and grabbed hold of me. He proceeded to sexually molest me and at the same time "talked filthy" into my ear. I was petrified. I can't begin to describe the feelings that I felt. I slapped his hands away and ran into the storage room, slamming the door behind me. I was trembling, crying, and I felt terrible. This was a time in my life when I was just starting to go through puberty, and I was very self-conscious about my body and the changes that were happening. I am having a hard time writing this because I told no one about it. I have kept this within until this year when I got involved in fighting pornography, and I told my husband what had happened to me. I remember being afraid to leave that storage room, so I stayed there. I was sure that my brother would be out in that hallway waiting for me to come out. My mother started calling for me and asking what was taking so long. I finally opened the door a bit, and saw that my brother was gone. While I ran toward the stairs, I noticed that my brother was back in his bedroom with his door shut.

I was too frightened to tell my mom. I felt dirty. I hated my body. I didn't want to grow up anymore. I wanted to hide and remain a child because [I believed] boys and men left children alone. I associated my sexual assault with part of growing up. I figured that was what happened to women all the time, and that men would always be trying to do horrible things to them. I didn't want to have a woman's body and I didn't want to ever get married.

From that day forward I made sure that I was never alone with my brother. Not only did he frighten me, but my father did also, even though my father never touched me the way that my brother did. I avoided being with my brother as much as possible. After a few months he had a girlfriend and stopped staring at me. But I couldn't forget everything. During the years I have had flashbacks, and I have experienced the same horrible feelings that I had experienced during my assault. I felt that I had done something wrong. I forgave my brother.

My brother was obsessed with *Playboy* magazines. There is no doubt in my mind that his obsession with these magazines led to his sexually assaulting me. Today, thankfully, he is a devout Christian, is active in church service, and has a small family. I am now 30 years old and I too have a family of my own. Since we live close, we often see each other. I have no idea if he even remembers what he did to me. If he does, he wants to forget it. I am trying to overcome my feelings of uneasiness around him. I know that he loves and cares for me. But the damage that was done to me has followed throughout my life. It has entered into my marriage and has had an effect on my relationship with my husband. But I love him, and he loves and understands me.

One thing that came out of this experience was a hearty hate for *Playboy* magazine. It hurt me; it hurt my brother. I felt when I was young that it turned all men into dirty-minded animals. Thank goodness that I had relationships with good men at that time. I was lucky in that I was able to associate my brother's actions with his dirty *Playboy* magazines. But others are not so lucky. I know how much that sexual assault damaged me. And it really upsets me to hear adults say, when they hear about a sexual assault, "good thing she wasn't raped, and that it was only a sexual assault." Yes, good thing, but many people dismiss sexual assaults as something trivial and not too bad. I can only say that they are horrible, and no one should have to experience them.

I also get upset when I hear people say that *Playboy* isn't a bad magazine; that it is harmless entertainment. In my experience this was not so. The *Playboy* copies that my brother had are now 15 years old, and those are considered mild today. I know there are probably many others who have gone through what I have because of this magazine.

Playboy is hardly the "harmless" publication which promoters would have us believe. And yet many of the leading companies in America, in addition to thousands of local "family" stores, keep helping *Playboy* and other pornographers push their products and their philosophy!

3.
A Psychologist's View of Pornography

By Dr. Victor Cline

Professor, Department of Psychology, the University of Utah

In 1984 a 21-year-old mother of two children entered Big Dan's Tavern in New Bedford, Massachusetts to buy a pack of cigarettes. She was seized by four male customers and repeatedly gang raped for two hours on a pool table. There were at least 15 other customers plus the bartender who witnessed her distress as she struggled and pleaded for help. However, no one summoned the police or gave her help of any kind.

This is reminiscent of Kitty Genovese, the Brooklyn girl, who some years ago was attacked, raped, and knifed to death in the interior court of her apartment building. This assault went on for over a half hour. Police later found, as they investigated, that 40 people were aware of the attack and her distress. Not one person attempted to give her assistance or even, anonymously, from the security of their apartments, bothered to call the police.

Several months ago the U.S. Surgeon General, Everett Koop, stated in an address to the American Academy of Pediatrics that violence is the nation's number one health problem—especially with people between the ages of 15 and 24—this is the group most decimated by violence of all kinds.

Violent Crime on Increase

The United States is by far the most violent country in the world compared with all of the other advanced societies. For example, the U.S. rape rate is many times higher than that of the United Kingdom. We have more homicides annually on just the island of Manhattan than those reported in all of England, Scotland, and troubled Ireland combined. Our homicide rate is ten times that of the Scandinavian countries. At the present time crimes of violence in the U.S. are increasing at four to five times the rate of population growth.

Behavioral scientists recognize that there are many causes for any violent act, and it behooves us to investigate and understand those key triggers or contributors—if we care at all about the kind of society we want for ourselves and our children. Many lines of evidence have pointed to media influences such as commercial cinema and television as being especially suspect; as presenting inappropriate models and instigations of violent and antisocial behavior, especially for our young.

Mental Health Study Blames TV Violence

In reviewing all of the scientific evidence relating to the effect TV violence has on behavior, the National Institute of Mental Health in 1984 issued a ten-year-report that concluded that there is in deed "overwhelming evidence of a causal relationship between violence on television and later aggressive behavior."

Some long-term studies and cross national studies also indicate that this learned aggressive behavior is stable over time—the victims stay aggressive. It is by no means just a transient kind of effect.

The reviewers of the research at the National Institute of Mental Health also note the role that TV (and by implication, commercial cinema) play as sex educators for our children. TV contributes significantly to sex role socialization as well as shaping attitudes and values about human sexuality. Various studies suggest that in TV presentations sex is commonly linked with violence. Erotic relationships are seldom seen as warm, loving, or stable. When sex is depicted it is almost always illicit. It is rather rare to suggest or depict sexual relations between a man and a woman married and who love each other. This agrees with similar results from my own research on the content of commercial cinema conducted several years ago.

Rape Rate Grows 700 Percent

Aggression against women is increasingly becoming a serious social problem. This can be seen in the escalation of wife battering, sexual molestation of female children, and sexual assaults on adult females.

Examining empirical data on the incidence of this type of thing is risky. This is because nearly all statistics on rape, for example, tend to underreport its actual occurrence. Many women for reasons of shame, humiliation, embarrassment, or seeking to avoid further trauma do not report these experiences. Data from many sources indicates that police get reports on one in four attempted or actual rapes. And of those reported less than 5 percent result in prosecution and conviction. Since 1933 the increase in the rape rate in the U.S. is in excess of 700 percent (this is in relation to population growth—in actual numbers the increase is much greater).

This means that the chances of a woman being sexually attacked are seven times greater now than in 1933. This clearly indicates major changes in male attitudes about sexual aggressiveness toward women. Obviously, more men today have a lower esteem of women. Why should this be in an age such as ours when women are being heard and winning rights?

Pornography Degrades Women

Feminists such as Susan Brownmiller, Diana Russell, Laura Lederer, and Kathleen Barry point to the fact that our culture influences men to regard women as things—to be used. They note, for example, that nearly all pornography is created by males for a primarily male audience. Most of it is hostile to women. There is much woman hatred in it. It is devoid of foreplay, tenderness, caring, to say nothing of love and romance.

They see its main purpose to humiliate and degrade the female body for the purpose of commercial entertainment, erotic stimulation, and pleasure for the male viewer. This is perceived as creating a cultural climate in which a rapist feels he is merely giving in to a normal urge and a woman is encouraged to believe that sexual masochism is healthy liberated fun.

Susan Brownmiller states, "Pornography, like rape, is a male invention designed to dehumanize women."

Many of the men's magazines such as *Hustler* are filled with antifemale messages both overt and covert. The victims in most "hard R" slasher movies are women—it is they who are most often sexually assaulted, tortured, and degraded. The feminist's concern is that these films sexually stimulate men while at the same time pairing this erotic arousal with images of violent assaults on women. The possibility of conditioning a potential male viewer into deviancy certainly has to be considered here.

Men Conditioned to Sexual Deviation
In a laboratory experiment using classical conditioning procedures at the Naudsley Hospital in London, England, Dr. Stanley Rachman conditioned a number of young males into being fetishists—a mild form of sexual deviation. A number of studies by such investigators as Davison, Bandura, Evans, Hackson, and McGuire suggest that deviant sexual fantasies through a process of masturbatory conditioning are related in many instances to later acted-out deviant sexual behavior. What happens here is that deviant sexual fantasies in the man's mind are paired with direct sexual stimulation and orgasm via masturbation. In this way the deviant fantasies acquire strong sexually arousing properties—which help sustain the sexual interest in the deviant behavior. Thus reinforced sexual imagery and thoughts (accompanied via masturbation) are a link in the acquisition and maintenance of new deviant sexual arousal and behavior. In the light of this, media portrayals of sex modeling male aggression against women logically can have a harmful effect on certain viewers. These portrayals, it would be concluded, facilitate deviant conditioning by providing new malignant fantasy material as well as

increasing motivation for masturbatory experiences—leading to changes in the man's sexual attitudes, appetites, and behavior.

For example: A Los Angeles firm is currently marketing an 8mm motion picture film, available through the mails to anybody wishing it, which depicts two girl scouts in their uniforms selling cookies from door to door. At one residence they are invited in by a mature, sexually aggressive male who proceeds to subject them to a variety of unusual and extremely explicit sexual acts— all shown in great detail. This film is what is usually referred to as "hard-core" pornography. If the research of Rachman, McGuire, and others has any meaning at all, it suggests that such a film could potentially condition some male viewers, via masturbatory conditioning, into fantasies and later behavior involving aggressive sex with female minors.

Also, we might mention, that sex therapists have for years used carefully selected erotic material to recondition men with sexual deviations and help them out of their problems. In other words, the conditioning can go both ways using erotic materials. If all sexual deviations are learned, as psychologist Albert Bandura suggests, then one would asssume that most deviations occur through "accidental conditioning"—which is exactly what many feminists have concerns about—especially as they see how they are treated in male-oriented media presentations.

At the present time in most urban areas of the U.S., there have arisen groups of women with concerns about what the media are doing to them—and especially about the social/sexual enculturation of males. Women Against Violence in Pornography and Media, based in San Francisco, is one example of this kind of group. Initially, their concerns were intuitive, moralistic, and emotional. They picketed various establishments—movie houses, adult bookstores, etc., selling or marketing highly sexist and antifemale materials—material that might tend to engender hate toward women. This includes the so-called "snuff films" in which women were supposedly murdered on-camera for the voyeuristic entertainment of male viewers.

However, in the last five years there has been a flood of well-done behavioral studies by researchers that appear to scientifically legitimize the concerns of these groups. These studies have repeatedly given documentation of potential harms to viewers of aggressive erotic materials, especially males.

These findings have been given very little attention by the popular press and are known only to a few scientists who are privy to the journals that these articles are showing up in. Thus, most ordinary citizens, journalists, as well as professionals in other disciplines, are not aware of these studies. For example, one of the editors of the *Utah Daily Chronicle* on March 1, 1985, in an editorial column discussing the cable TV bills before our state legislature, wrote, "Research has shown there is no demonstrable relationship between watching TV and increased aggressiveness . . . [and] regardless of what Utah legislators may believe, there is no scientific correlation between obscenity and antisocial conduct."

Both of these statements are totally incorrect. I am sure they were written as a result of ignorance, not as a conscious attempt at deception. In fact, quite ironically, on the day this editorial appeared, the Department of Psychology was sponsoring a widely publicized seminar featuring one of the nation's leading authorities on television effects, Dr. Raoul Huesmann, who discussed a pioneering 22-year study on the long-term negative effects of TV violence viewing.

World's Most Violent Advanced Society

I will not further belabor the issue of media violence and its potential negative effects on viewers. The evidence is really quite overwhelming on this issue. But let me briefly summarize what the literature suggests:

(1) We are the most violent advanced society in the world.

(2) We have the highest rates of media violence (in our entertainments) of any nation.

(3) There are something like 20 years of behavioral studies linking exposure to media violence with violent behavior. These include both laboratory and field studies. And while there are many contributions to any particular violent act, I do not think that any fair reviewer of the literature can deny that the media are

one important contributor to the violence problems in our society.

In my judgment repeated violence viewing also desensitizes the observer to the pathology in the film or material witnessed. It becomes with repeated viewing more acceptable and tolerable. We lose the capacity to empathize with the victim. Man's inhumanity to man (or woman) becomes a spectator sport. We develop and cultivate an appetite for it, no different than in early Rome, where people watched gladiatorial contests in which men fought to their deaths, dismembering their opponents' bodies. In other contests, others fought wild animals bare-handed, eventually to be eaten alive. Again, a spectator sport. We become to some extent debased, even dehumanized, if you wish, by participating in these kinds of experiences. And, of course, approximations of what happened in the Roman arena nightly occur in some movie houses and on some TV screens—especially the cable variety where explicit violence is broadcast unedited. And usually—women are the victims.

Increasing Assaults in Marriage

Let us now move to the issue of linking aggressive pornography to increased aggressive behavior in marriage. It can be physical abuse, psychological abuse, or both. I see many couples in marital counseling. Violence between spouses is a common problem. Of course many women have learned to fight back. And this leads to an ever-escalating exchange of anger and hostility. Divorce usually doesn't solve the problem. If you don't know how to handle anger and aggressive feelings in one relationship, switching partners doesn't necessarily solve that problem for you in the next relationship.

There have been many experiments on aggressive pornography and its effects on consumers conducted by such capable investigators as Edward Donnerstein and Leonard Berkowitz at the University of Wisconsin; Neil Malamuth and James Check at the University of Manitoba; Dolf Zillman and Jennings Bryant at Indiana University; and Seymour Feshback and his associates at UCLA.

Sexual Arousal, Aggression Linked

There has been a convergence of evidence from many sources suggesting that sexual arousal and aggression are linked or are mutually enhancing. Thus materials that are sexually exciting can stimulate aggressive behavior and, contrariwise, portrayals of aggression in books, magazines, and films can raise some people's levels of sexual arousal.

Thus it is not by accident that some four-letter words are frequently used in the context of an epithet or as part of a verbal attack on another.

Many theorists have noted the intimate relationship between sex and aggression—including Sigmund Freud, or more recently, Robert Stoler at UCLA who suggests that frequently it is hostility that generates and enhances sexual excitement.

A large number of research studies consistently and repetitiously keep coming to one conclusion—those subjects who are sexually aroused by strong erotic stimuli show significantly greater aggression than nonaroused controls.

The typical experiment will sexually arouse with pornographic stimuli a group of experimental subjects who will then be given an opportunity to punish a confederate with electric shock. Their aggressiveness will be compared to a neutral group who will have seen only a bland nonsexual film or reading material.

If the film combines both erotic *and* aggressive elements, this usually produces even higher levels of aggressiveness (as measured by the subjects' willingness to shock their partners at even higher and apparently more painful levels of shock intensity). If the erotic material is very mild—like pin-ups and cheesecake type photos—then it appears to have reverse effect on aggression—tending to dampen it.

In the situation of reading about or witnessing a filmed presentation of rape, if the female victim is seen as in great pain this can also have a dampening effect on aggressive arousal. It serves as an inhibitor. But if the portrayal showing the woman as finally succumbing to and enjoying the act (as is typical of most pornography), then the situation is reversed for males (but not females). It becomes very arousing. For men, the fantasy of a woman becoming sexually excited as a result of a sexual assault reverses any inhibitions that might have been initially mobilized by the coercive nature of the act and seeing the woman initially in pain.

This message—that pain and humiliation can be "fun"—encourages in men the relaxation of inhibitions against rape.

Doctrs Gager and Schurr in their studies on the causes of rape note that a common theme in pornography is that women enjoy being raped and sexually violated. Sexual sadism is presented as a source of sexual pleasure for women. The Gager and Schurr studies note: "The pattern rarely changes in the porno culture. . . . After a few preliminary skirmishes, women invite or demand further violation, begging male masters to rape them into submission, torture, and violence. In this fantasy land, females wallow in physical abuse and degradation. It is a pattern of horror which we have seen in our examination of sex cases translated again and again into actual assaults."

University Study Shows Effects of Movies
Going outside the laboratory, Neal Malamuth at the University of Manitoba sent hundreds of students to movies playing in the community. He wanted to see what the effects would be of their being exposed to films portraying sexual violence as having positive consequences. The movies they went to see were not pornography, but everyday "sex and violence" of the R-rated variety. The films included *Swept Away* (about a violent male agressor and a woman who learns to crave sexual sadism; they find love on a deserted island). A second film, *The Getaway*, tells about a woman who falls in love with the man who raped her in front of her husband, then both taunt the husband until he commits suicide.

A second group of students was assigned to see two control films, *A Man and a Woman,* and *Hooper,* both showing tender romance and nonexplicit sex. Within a week of seeing the films, Malamuth administered an attitude survey to all students who had participated in the experiment. The students did not know that the survey had anything to do with the films which they had seen. Embedded within the survey were questions of such relating to acceptance of interpersonal violence and acceptance of such rape myths as "women enjoy being raped." Examples of questions asked also included: "Many women have an unconscious wish to be raped and may unconsciously set up a situation in which they are likely to be attacked."

The results of the survey indicated that exposure to the films portraying sexual violence significantly increased male subjects' acceptance of interpersonal violence against women. For females, the trend was in the opposite direction.

Dr. Malamuth concluded: "The present findings constitute the first demonstration in a nonlaboratory setting . . . of relatively long-term effects of movies that fuse sexuality and violence." And, of course, these were not hard-core pornography but rather R-rated type, edited films that have appeared on national commercial TV and unedited films shown on cable TV.

As I review the literature on media effects, it appears that in the areas of both sex and violence materials depicting these kinds of behaviors do several things: (1) they stimulate and arouse aggressive and sexual feelings—especially in males; (2) they show or instruct in detail *how* to do the acts—much of it antisocial; (3) when seen frequently enough have a desensitization effect which reduces feelings of conscience, guilt, inhibitions, or inner controls, the act is in a sense legitimized by its repetitious exposure; and finally, (4) there is increased likelihood that the individual will act out what he has witnessed.

Seymour Feshbach's research at UCLA has a direct bearing on this issue. After exposing a group of male college students to a sadomasochistic rape story taken from *Penthouse* magazine— telling of a woman's pleasure at being sexually mistreated—he asked these men if they would like to emulate what the rapist did to the woman. Seventeen percent said they would. When asked the same question but with the added assurance they would not get caught—51 percent indicated a likelihood of raping. This finding has been replicated in a number of other studies—though the percentages vary somewhat from research to research.

Doctors Edward Donnerstein and Neil Malamuth, in reviewing a large number of both field and laboratory experiments, found that exposure to media materials that mix both sex and violence causes six things to happen: (1) it sexually excites and arouses (especially) the male viewer; (2) it increases both his aggressive *attitudes* and *behavior;* (3) it stimulates the production of aggressive rape fantasies; (4) it increases men's acceptance of so-called rape myths (such as: "women ask for it"); (5) it produces a lessened sensitivity about rape (and increased callousness); and (6) it leads to men admitting an increased possiblity of themselves raping someone—especially if they think they can get away with it.

Pornography Reduces Compassion

What about exposure to nonaggressive erotic materials? Do these have any kind of effects on the consumer? Doctors Dolf Zillman and Jennings Bryant at Indiana University studied 160 male and female undergraduates who were divided into groups where they were exposed to: (1) massive amounts of pornography over a period of six weeks; (2) a moderate amount of pornography over that time period; and (3) no exposure over the same time period. Among their many findings were that being exposed to a lot of pornography led to a desensitization effect. The more they saw, the less offensive and objectionable it became to them. They also tended to see rape as a more trivial offense. They had an increasing loss of compassion for women as rape victims (even though no aggressive pornography was shown them).

Massive exposure to nonaggressive pornography clearly promoted sexual callousness in males toward women generally. This was measured by a scale where men agreed with such items as: "Pickups should expect to put out." Or, "If they are old enough to bleed, they are old enough to butcher" (referring to women).

The thrust of this presentation is to suggest that there is an abundance of scientific evidence suggesting social harms from some types of media exposure as has been previously discussed. The studies we have discussed are only illustrative. Many others have not been mentioned due to time limitations. Extensive documentation and lengthy bibliographies on this subject matter are available from the speaker on request.

Can We Control Pornography?

We now come to the really hot issue—the bottom line. Does a community have a constitutional right through democratically enacted laws to censor or limit the public broadcast of these kinds of materials—because of their malignant nature? The recent controversy about the First Amendment of the Constitution? Where does or where can one draw the line? How bad or pathological does material have to be before it can be limited? Or should our position be: anything goes regardless of the consequences? Free speech is free speech.

Seymour Feshbach, the UCLA psychologist, states: "As psychologists, we would support community efforts to restrict violence in erotica to adults who are fully cognizant of the nature of the material and who choose knowingly to buy it. We are opposed to advertisements that have appeared in some popular magazines depicting sadomasochism; a recent fashion layout in *Vogue*, for instance, featured a man brutally slapping an attractive woman. We also oppose the practice of some therapists who try to help their patients overcome sexual inhibitions by showing them films of rape or by encouraging them to indulge in rape fantasies. Psychologists, in our judgment, ought not to support, implicitly or explicitly, the use and dissemination of violent erotic materials."

In reference to the First Amendment to our Constitution, we must recognize that today there are many kinds of democratically enacted prohibitions of speech and expression. These, of course, can be amended or repealed anytime we wish. Examples include libel, slander, perjury, conspiracy, false advertising, excitement to violence or speech that might create a "clear and present danger" such as yelling "Fire!" in a crowded theater. Still other examples include TV cigarette advertisements and also obscenity. In fact most of the people who went to jail in the Watergate scandal did so because of what they said—or for words they spoke (e.g., perjury and conspiracy).

In certain public broadcast mediums such as TV and radio, even obscene language can be proscribed without running afoul of the First Amendment.

At present, cable TV is the most controversial area about what is appropriate or inappropriate for broadcast. Currently there are virtually no restrictions on what can be aired. There are some channels in the U.S. broadcasting the roughest kind of hard-core pornography. There are others, including some in Utah, that are regularly broadcasting soft-core pornography mixed with violence. Last spring one of the local cable networks broadcast some 15 times *Eyes of a Stranger*. This film shows in explicit detail a young woman and her boyfriend being attacked by a sadist. He chops the boyfriend's head off, then proceeded to tear the girl's clothes off, strangle her, then rapes the dead body. The film continues with a series of attacks, rapes, and killings of other females. In my judgment this kind of programming, some of it in primetime, represents antisocial and irresponsible behavior on the part of the cable station owners.

Of course, there are many other similar type films which are being regularly broadcast. This is not an isolated incident. But along with this are films of great merit and quality which represent a major contribution to our cultural life as well as entertainment.

At present close to 30 percent of homes in the U.S. have cable. Industry analysts project that by 1985 this will be up to 50 percent and by the end of the decade 80-90 percent. This means that within a few years most all of us will have cable. This is not hard to understand when you consider that very shortly the cable networks will be able to outbid the regular networks for choice sporting events, fights, new Broadway musicals, etc. Even now all the latest movies come to cable before they reach regular commercial TV.

At present there is a double standard in television. The FCC (Federal Communications Commission) has control over the broadcast of appropriate materials by the regular commercial TV channels. They cannot air obscene or other objectionable material without threat of losing their licenses. Cable TV has no restrictions whatever. And, of course, cable firms are taking advantage of this. And there are some adults in our community who are delighted. Others are appalled and have concerns, especially about exposing their children to this kind of programming.

As with most controversial issues, there are no simple solutions which will please everybody. But somewhere a line must be drawn—if we care about the quality of life in our community. We have a right to protect ourselves in our own self-interest.

Media Savagery Grows

George Elliot has commented: "If one is for civilization, for being civilized . . . , then one must be willing to take a middle way and pay the price for responsibility. To be civilized, to accept authority, to rule with order, costs deep in the soul, and not the least of what it costs is likely to be some of the sensuality of the irresponsible." Some have argued, as Elliot notes, that since guilt reduces pleasure in sex, the obvious solution is to abolish all sexual taboos and liberate pornography, which in turn would supposedly free the human spirit—and the body.

This is a cheery optimistic view, not unlike the sweet hopefulness of the old-fashioned anarchist who thought that all we had to do in order to attain happiness was to get rid of governments so that we might all express our essentially good nature unrestrained. But sexual anarchism, or the aggressive impulse turned loose, like political anarchism before it, is a "lovely" but fraudulent daydream. Perhaps, before civilization, savages were noble, but if there is anything we have learned in this century, it is that those who regress from civilization become ignoble beyond all toleration. They may aspire to innocent savagery, but what they achieve too often is brutality and loss of their essential humanity.

The issue of how we should deal with the savagery which continues to escalate in our media presentations is just as much your problem as mine. I have shared with you some of the consequences of its presence on our culture. But the solution has to be a shared one—if we really believe in democracy.

4.
How Pornography Fuels
Child Sexual Abuse

In Hilliard, Ohio in the summer of 1985, police charged a local juvenile with two counts of rape and another youth with two counts of complicity in connection with the rape of a ten-year-old retarded youth. The victim was in the town park in the company of the two who were charged when they decided to take advantage of him sexually. Another youth witnessed the acts but did not take part. All were males ranging in age from 9-11 years.

When the retarded child refused to consent to engage in oral sex, one of the boys beat him with a stick until he submitted. The 11-year-old then assaulted him both orally and anally. Police investigating the incident found pornographic literature under the amphitheater stage where the incident occurred. The boy who raped the retarded child had been reading pornographic magazines.

"I've been in law enforcement for 18 years, and I've never seen a homosexual rape between two boys so young before," said Hilliard Police Lt. Ron Bush. Bush said all of the boys are from good families whose parents work hard and care for their children.

Child pornography and child sexual abuse—only a perverted mind would not be willing to agree that these things simply should not be tolerated. How big a role does so-called "adult

pornography'' play in child pornography and child sexual abuse?
A great deal more than the producers of adult pornography will
ever admit.

The following article appeared in the *Dallas Morning News*
during March 1985:

Two Dallas boys, ages eight and nine, were being held for
questioning for alleged sexual assault of a six-year-old girl.
The little girl had a tear in her cervix. The assault was
serious and brutal.

Rape crisis officials said the incident was one of a
growing number of sexual assaults on children by other
children. Jan Delipsey of the Dallas County Rape Crisis
Center said that she had recently had a case in which a five-
year-old boy sexually assaulted a three-year-old.

Ms. Delipsey said that, of the 40 or 50 cases of sexual
assault involving children each month, three to six cases
involved children under the age of 12 who had sexually
abused other children. The eight-year-old Dallas boy began
abusing boys and girls in the neighborhood after he saw
some pornographic movies, said the victim's mother.

In Cleveland, Ohio a counselor for a preschool program has
been charged with three felonies for allegedly taking a ten-year-
old girl to his apartment, showing her sexually explicit videotapes, and fondling her.

An assistant dean at a medical center in New York was
recently arrested on a charge of sexually assaulting a ten-year-old
girl in a Chicago hotel. Chicago police said the 45-year-old man
was arrested early in the morning and told them he was teaching
the girl about sex education. Police found a 35mm camera along
with a number of pornographic pictures. The girl said later that
the New York man had assaulted her in past visits to Chicago.

"Candyman"
A 56-year-old electrical engineer gave neighborhood children in
Clarkston, Georgia candy to come into his apartment and view a

videotape. The children called him "Candyman." He pled guilty to two counts of child molestation and five counts of enticing a child for indecent purposes.

An assistant district attorney said all the children had been too scared to tell their parents about the "Candyman" because they thought they would get in trouble for what they had seen.

Someone sent me a newspaper clipping that tells of a 78-year-old man being charged with sexually abusing an eight-year-old girl. Pornographic books, magazines, and video cassettes—some depicting young children involved in sex—were seized at the man's home. Indications were that the elderly offender would be charged with crimes of sexual abuse of other children.

In Dothan, Alabama police arrested a 56-year-old man and charged him with enticing a child for immoral purposes, including rape and sodomizing a seven-year-old Dothan girl. Police discovered thousands of pornographic pictures involving children after searching the man's home. "We also found pornographic storybooks [featuring] Mother Goose, Snow White, and Cinderella," said Police Sgt. Jackie Mendheim.

A 55-year-old substitute teacher was charged in Waukegan, Illinois in a child pornography and sexual assault case after police found more than 10,000 photographs of nude children in his house. Lt. Philip Joiner, spokesman for the Waukegan Police Department, said that officers found the man's home "literally wallpapered" with nude photographs of children, mostly girls ages 7-14.

Suitcases filled with children's underwear were found in a closet. Each piece of underwear was wrapped in cellophane and tagged with names and dates as far back as 1966. The offender had a two-way mirror mounted in his bathroom through which he took pictures of the children.

A Waukegan school official said the teacher frequently preached to students, quoting Bible passages about morality and profanity. "He did an effective job, but he was a religious nut," the official said.

A 48-year-old psychiatrist in Milwaukee, already on probation for sexually assaulting a boy in Florida, was arrested for importing child pornography. In 1979 the man was convicted in Orange County Circuit Court in Orlando for a lewd assault on a male child. He was placed on 15 years' probation. In February 1984 customs agents in Chicago began seizing a series of pornographic materials that depicted children and that were addressed to the psychiatrist's apartment. When authorities searched the apartment, they found more than 100 magazines, more than 200 photographs, and six video cassettes depicting children in sexually explicit poses.

A ten-year-old boy in London, England was recently arrested and charged with raping a 12-year-old girl. London officers say the child is the youngest rape suspect they have ever arrested. Police said that after they talked with his parents and took the boy into custody, they searched his room. They found dozens of pornographic magazines and nude photos.

A psychiatrist who examined the boy said that the child told him he got his ideas from reading magazines with pictures of nude men and women. "He said he wanted to be like the men he saw in the magazines and on TV," the psychiatrist commented.

Sells Daughter for $3,000
Undercover agents of the Kentucky attorney general's office paid a man $3,000 outside the Gateway Motel in Covington, Kentucky. They had made a deal with him to use his three-year-old daughter for "pornographic and sexual" purposes. The 27-year-old father and his 18-year-old girlfriend were charged with soliciting to commit rape, promoting prostitution, use of a minor in a sexual performance, and other sex offenses.

In Philadelphia 12 men were charged for committing sex crimes against juveniles. As is so often the case, pornography was also involved. Some 4,000 photographic prints, slides, and films were seized. The collection would be worth about half a million dollars on the kiddie pornography black market.

A 45-year-old Denver man attracted single mothers who felt their sons needed a good "father figure." He operated a figurine business and hired young boys, apparently to help him run display booths.

But the man was arrested in August 1985 on suspicion of exploiting and molesting young boys. Hundreds of explicit pornographic photographs, 8mm films, and slides were confiscated from his apartment.

Again, pornography *is* a factor in child sexual abuse. Child sexual abuse has become an all-pervasive problem in our society. The use of children as sex objects is a national disgrace in America!

How Serious Is the Problem?

Dr. Frederick Green at Children's Hospital in Washington, D.C. says that more children are brought to the hospital because of sexual abuse than because of broken bones or for tonsillectomies. Dr. Carl Rogers, also at Children's Hospital, says that over half of these sexually abused children are younger than nine years old.

Estimates are overwhelming: anywhere between 600,000 and 1,200,000 children are sexually abused and drawn into the world of child pornography every year. Estimates vary because experts believe that from 50 percent to 80 percent of cases of child sexual abuse are never reported.

Although kiddie pornography is not readily available over the counter, organizations exist nationwide for the buying and trading of hard-core child pornography.

On May 21, 1984 in the act of signing the Child Protection Act of 1984, President Reagan remarked: "We've taken some other initiatives in the antipornography effort. Last year the Customs Service increased its seizures of obscene materials coming in across our borders by over 200 percent. Sixty percent of the material was child pornography."

The *New York Times* on April 13, 1984 quoted Justice Department studies that "thousands of children under 18 years of age are killed annually by repeat murderers who prey sexually on children and by adults involved in child prostitution and pornography."

Even as early as 1977 the Los Angeles Police Department estimated that as many as 30,000 boys and girls were sexaully exploited by adults in that city every year. In that same year in New York City, officials estimated that 120,000 children were sexually exploited.

Today's problem is compounded by organizations now openly advocating sexual abuse of children. The Rene Guyon Society based in California boasts 8,500 members who espouse the motto "Sex by eight or it's too late." The eastern equivalent, the North American Man/Boy Love Association (NAMBLA), active in 11 major cities in the Northeast and Midwest, advocates total abolition of the "age of consent" laws relating to sexual intercourse between adult and child (mostly man and boy).

The British equivalent, the Paedophiliac Information Exchange (PIE), suggests four as the age of consent. These are no longer isolated lunatic fringe movements. NAMBLA was featured last year on the *Donahue* show. The problem is beyond the serious stage. It is critical!

Magazines for Sick Minds

"Pornographic exploitation of children," according to Dr. Shirley O'Brien, author of *Child Pornography*, "makes people react in one of five different ways: the first person has never heard of it; the second says, "Live and let live"; the third becomes sick, angry, and motivated to action; the fourth profiteers from it; and the fifth is sexually excited by it."

Child pornography—often referred to as "kiddie porn"—was virtually unknown two decades ago. Dr. Ann Burgess, of the University of Pennsylvania School of Nursing, says that there are now nearly 280 magazines on the market dealing with child pornography, and of these, 275 are published monthly. In these editions there are estimated to be 800 to 1,000 additional suppliers of child pornography for sale to the subscribers.

Included in a Department of Justice study was an assessment of the current state of the child-porno industry:

In the past decade, hundreds of thousands of children have been swallowed up by the child pornography industry. Child pornography has become a highly organized, multimillion dollar industry whose products are distributed through an informal but close-knit network nationwide. While estimates concerning the number of children involved in child pornography are difficult to verify and the facts and figures vary, one thing is very clear: a significant number of children are being sexually exploited throughout the country. The majority of children recruited into child pornography are often runaways, from broken homes, or generally neglected children who range from 7 to 14 years old.

Due to large quantities of pornography confiscated by police officers during child molestation arrests, many law enforcement agencies see a clear and direct relationship between pornography and sexual molestation of children.

One example: A Tennessee man was indicted on charges of using minors for obscene purposes and aggravated rape. The grand jury which indicted him was convened after authorities discovered pornographic pictures of children, books on child sex, and sexual paraphernalia at the man's home. Investigators found about 1,000 sexually explicit photos of more than 40 girls, ranging in age from 3 to 12, at the residence of the offender.

In the *Report to the Attorney General on Child Pornography*, the California Attorney General's Advisory Committee on Obscenity and Pornography noted:

In interviews with a great many police officers, the Committee was frequently told: "I never arrested a child molester who did not have pornography in his possession. . . . "
Also, a Los Angeles Police Department investigation studied over 40 child molestation cases during a five-month period and interviewed more than 100 victims and suspects. Pornography was found to be present in *every* case.

Child sexual abuse has increased as adult pornography has increased in the past few years. The evidence is clearly overwhelming.

These Are Real Children

Typical of a child-sex abuse scenario was a case in Mississippi. A note left by a 12-year-old girl who ran away from home triggered an investigation by city, county, and state officials that led to the arrest of a man on a child-molesting charge. In his home police found a 38-caliber pistol under a mattress and "quite a bit of pornographic material," according to police.

The 12-year-old victim said that the man had sexually abused her on a regular basis. Police said the girl was afraid to talk about it.

Another typical case involved a sex-abuse artist in Florida. Authorities arrested a man in Lake Park in January for filming and photographing girls age 8 to 16 in the nude.

Vice agents found in the man's photography studio various films, photographs, video cassette tapes, and voice cassettes as well as cameras, recorders, and televisions, "all used in filming the incidents."

Also found in the studio, according to the sheriff's office, were "hundreds and hundreds of books and magazines like *Playboy* and *Penthouse* . . . plus some publications dealing only with child pornography."

Child Pornography Rings Discovered

In a major study on child sexual abuse, social scientists have uncovered evidence of child sex rings in the "kiddie porno" world. The study shows that adults who head the rings play on the normal interests of young children. The adults involve the children in secret societies to which they become tied by bonds of threats and fear.

Dr. Ann Burgess headed the group which released a study based on two years of interviews with 62 children. The children, who averaged 11 years of age, had been involved in a total of 11 sex rings in the Northeast and Midwest from 1973 to 1981 for periods ranging from a few months to four years. The children and their parents, who were also interviewed, agreed to cooperate in the research project after being referred for counseling by the police or courts.

All the rings had adult leaders. Some of the rings not only used children sexually, but also produced and sold pornographic pictures of the children engaged in sex acts. Leaders used peer pressure as well as threats to keep children from telling their parents.

In all the rings, adult pornography was used to instruct the children. The children were victims of a carefully orchestrated seduction often relying on sex, drugs, alcohol, and peer pressures.

In a typical sex ring described by Dr. Burgess, "a 54-year-old man who had received a community award for devoting 25 years to the youth of the community as a basketball coach was arrested by Federal agents for distributing child pornography. Most of the 17 boys in his sex ring had been recruited from the ages of 10 to 12.

"At after-school meetings at the man's house, a sexual ritual was enacted which began with the boys sitting in a circle drinking beer and smoking marijuana and the ring leader speaking in a monotone. Then, while drum music played, the man would leap from behind a curtain wearing a Samurai outfit. That signaled the boys to begin sexual activities which the man would photograph. At the end of the ritual, one of the boys would have sex relations with the man."

Sgt. Ray Micknowski, of the sexual assault section of the Pittsburgh Police Department, told a Senate subcommittee that child sex abusers often use pornographic materials to "show a child what to do."

From his own experience dealing with sex offenders, Sergeant Micknowski said the child may need reassurance before he or she is persuaded to cooperate with the sex abuser. So the offender will show him or her pornographic photos. He has the child pose for pornographic photos by showing photos in which other children have posed nude.

A New York man who sexually abused children pleaded not responsible to the charges. He was charged with molesting three children over a year-long period.

On a calendar, the offender kept a detailed record of the

various sex acts he performed on three children—two brothers and their sister.

At the time of the man's arrest, police seized from his home hundreds of sexually explicit items, including movies, photo albums, and magazines.

Testimony before the Senate Subcommittee on Investigations revealed that a worldwide network of child pornographers exists. The network includes sex tours and auctions, with few efforts by governments to stop the activity. Net profits are estimated in the area of $5 billion annually.

According to a report in the *New York Daily News*, testimony stated that "children as young as 18 months are brutalized, bought, sold, swapped, and photographed in obscene displays."

Penn's Dr. Burgess, recognized nationally as an expert in the field, believes sexual abuse of children and child pornography are problems that need to be publicized so that people will be stirred to action that will protect children and deal appropriately with offenders.

In a treatment program she directs for child pornography victims, Dr. Burgess said recently that the youngest sexual abuser she had treated was a nine-year-old boy who raped a three-year-old girl. The nine-year-old had been taught how by a 16-year-old.

Alfred S. Regnery, administrator of the Office of Juvenile Justice and Delinquency and Prevention, Washington, D.C., says that as many as 6,000 children are murdered each year in this nation. Regnery's office is a part of the U.S. Justice Department.

It is believed that a substantial number of those 6,000 murdered children are both physically and sexually abused by their murderers. Almost two million children run away from home each year. Ninety percent return home, but the 200,000 who do not go back home, for the most part, support themselves by prostitution, pornography, drugs, and sex. They are led into the illegal sex and drug business by adults who feed on pornography.

Kenneth V. Lanning, the FBI's child sexual abuse and pornography specialist, says sexual victimization of children is the most underreported serious crime in the country. In six years, 1976 to 1982, cases of child sexual abuse reported to government protection agencies increased 649 percent, from 7,559 to 56,607.

"By even the most conservative estimates, a child is sexually abused someplace within the United States every two minutes," Sen. Christopher J. Dodd said in addressing a session of the Senate Children's Caucus.

Pedophiles—people who are sexually aroused by viewing nude children—are not just little old men in raincoats, says Robert D. Joy, chief of the U.S. Postal Service branch that investigates child pornography mailings. Police are uncovering more and more cases of what they call perverse child porn— painful experiences resulting when children are tied with chains and ropes.

Those who sexually abuse children are likely to repeat their offenses according to psychologists and child welfare specialists. The FBI recently uncovered a nationwide ring that specialized in abducting young children and selling them for purposes of sex and pornography. The ring accepted orders from customers based on height, weight, and hair color and furnished them with "special order children" as young as three.

Some specialists contend that pedophiles can rarely be "cured" or rehabilitated. Consequently, for many the only solution is one of desperation—lock them up and throw away the key.

Others, however, see it differently. They see hope for the pedophile who seeks proper help. Detective Joel Johnson investigates child pornography and sexual exploitation cases for the Norman Police Department in the Oklahoma City metropolitan area. He approaches the pedophile phenomenon from the Christian perspective. Johnson accepts the usual professional assessment that the pedophile is "sick," but he goes a step further to say, "It is a sin problem, being a slave to sin." Johnson contends that many pedophiles choose to continue abusing children ". . . instead of getting right with God."

In a study for the FBI, Dr. Burgess identified the profile of a pedophile: he usually seeks groups of children; often he uses his job to gain access to children and authority over them.

Johnson confirmed the first point, saying that an appreciable number of pedophiles cold-bloodedly attempt to become a part of church groups and activities, Big Brothers organizations, Scouts, or other groups in which children participate.

Dr. Edward F. Zigler, professor of psychology at Yale University, cites the entertainment industry as a contributing factor in child sexual abuse because the industry promotes youth as objects of sexual desire. Dr. Zigler is a former chief of U.S. Children's Bureau in the U.S. Department of Health and Human Services.

Dr. Zigler names several characteristics commonly found in known pedophiles. First, he says the molesters are generally immature, without feelings of guilt, responsibility, or social obligation. Second, very few of the offenders seek help on their own. Those forced into treatment usually lack the maturity to control their own actions. Third, most pedophiles do not perceive themselves as having a problem. "A person must want to be helped for therapy to be successful," Zigler points out.

A fourth characteristic often found among pedophiles but not named by Zigler is the offender's tie to pornography. Pornography—its production or its use to lure children into sexual acts—often hovers just below the surface of child sexual abuse. Lt. John T. Dugan, Jr. of the Buffalo, New York Police Department says it is rare if pornography is *not* involved in the sexual abuse of children.

One victim of childhood incest told me there were always "dirty" books around the house when he was growing up, and he thought for years that incest was the normal family pattern. Another victim told me a similar story, first of incest and later of marital problems clearly connected to the pornographic literature read by the offenders involved.

Detective Johnson outlined the steps often followed by a pedophile who begins with "soft-core" child pornography. Exposure to this "child erotica" desensitizes as dehumanizes and leads to tolerance. Tolerance leads to a desire for more and more bizarre and perverted child pornography. A compulsion to collect the material develops and the pedophile is literally addicted—quite comparable to the addiction suffered by one addicted to drugs.

The collecting of child pornography and the abuse of children apparently go hand in hand, each aspect provoking and encouraging the other. According to Johnson, it is not at all unusual for the pedophile to possess a cache of pornography worth from $5,000 to $20,000 at current street value.

"Pedophiles are skilled at the seduction process," Dr. Burgess said. "Often pornography is used to lower the child's inhibitions, to show the child what to do."

Most pedophiles repeat their offenses many times, abusing many children. Johnson says most authorities agree that in the life of the average pedophile, more than 60 children will suffer abuse. He finds that figure consistent with the pedophile cases he himself has dealt with. Dr. A. Nicholas Groth, prison psychologist, sets the number at 67. Groth has worked with hundreds of convicted sex offenders in an innovative treatment program at the state prison, Somers, Connecticut.

A most tragic aspect of this statistic is highlighted by Dr. Burgess who says that once abused, children continue to have problems. "They think about it a lot. They can't do their school work and they can't play with friends," says Burgess.

In Harris County, Texas, a man who was imprisoned in 1982 for raping a child had been on parole only three months when he was charged this spring with the rape of a four-year-old girl. The man, sentenced to four years in prison on June 28, 1982, had served less than half of his sentence when he was released to repeat his crime.

Ronald Luchau, 53, of Phoenix, Arizona was given a maximum sentence for his involvement in the recent sex abuse of five young brothers and sisters. Luchau is a five-time convicted sex offender.

Judge William J. Burke, in sentencing Luchau, said, "I feel no pangs of mercy in my heart for you." Luchau's victims were sisters five and six years old and their brothers, 10, 13, and 15. The victims' mother also has been convicted in the case and the father awaits trial.

An Erie County, New York man was given five years' probation and fined $5,000 in 1980 for taking lewd photographs of an eight-year-old girl who came to his home to play with his children. Released early from probation in June 1984 because he was leading a "stable" life, he was arrested again in November for child sexual abuse.

A New Jersey man, paroled after serving only nine months of a five-year sentence for child molestation, was arrested again recently on charges of sexually molesting an eight-year-old girl. The 62-year-old man was first arrested in 1982 on charges of molesting three young children. He was released in September 1984 and arrested again in the spring of 1985 on charges of attacking the eight-year-old girl.

The list could go on indefinitely.

The mother of a ten-year-old girl who was one of the offender's victims complained bitterly about his parole saying, "My daughter was traumatized by what happened to her. It was two years ago but she still has nightmares and is frightened to go outside and play. . . . They should lock that monster up and throw away the key."

Surprisingly, some experts such as Dr. Zigler seem to agree. "Sexual psychopaths," says Zigler, "are very low-level people. The prognosis for these people is pretty poor at best. They are best in the hands of the criminal justice system."

The problem with that solution, however, is twofold. First, a part of their sentence is almost certain to include psychological treatment. But these offenders often defy attempts at treatment because they do not desire treatment. Second, when convicted, they do not normally serve their full sentences before being released to continue their crimes.

Instead of wringing their hands and shaking their heads in disbelief at the epidemic, the "experts" might be well advised to consider the solution of faith combined with therapy illustrated by a child abuser who shared his story with me.

When he was seven, two older boys sexually assaulted him. Only a year later, his own brother forced him to participate in perverted sex. Like many other such victims, as an adult, he became a pedophile, that is, a child sex abuser.

"Through these experiences," he wrote recently, "I found myself molesting most of my nieces. . . . When they were old enough to know better, I turned to children in my neighborhood."

His family learned of his sexual perversion, but insisted that the problem be "swept under the rug" so he still could not seek treatment. Eventually, he became too tired and desperate to continue his double life—trying to be a Christian and yet molesting children. He *asked* one of his victims to report him.

He has served more than half of a ten-year sentence, and has appeared several times before the parole board. Although he has had a place to live, a job, and counseling lined up each time, his parole has always been denied. A Christian halfway house and his pastor are standing ready to assist him when he is paroled.

His letter concluded: "Most people say pedophiles cannot be cured. I say that's a lie, as I believe with proper therapy and my Lord Jesus Christ, anyone can learn to control this illness and keep it from ever happening again.

"Please share with your listeners, there *is* help for a sex offender! Jesus Christ and therapy can make this happen! Please remember me in your prayers for God's direction."

Children in Glossy Pornography

Pornography dealing with child sexual abuse is no longer limited to low-budget, backroom productions. *Penthouse, Playboy,* and *Hustler,* some of the largest sellers in the pornography market, have gotten into the act in recent years.

What kind of material do these and other magazines contain? A *Playboy* magazine featured a cartoon in which a little girl is coming out of a man's apartment. She is putting her clothes on following a sexual encounter with the man who is standing in the doorway in a bathrobe. She turns to the man and says, "You call *that* being molested?"

Penthouse for May 1984 carried an article in the "erotic encounters" section—the section designed to stimulate malignant fantasies—about a man's sexual encounter with his young niece. He told of spanking her until "my hand was stinging so badly I couldn't continue." Oral and other sex acts were described with violence abounding. The uncle stated, "I could sense she was enjoying her punishment and that her defiance and pleading were only an act. . . . She was moaning and crying with the intense feelings of pleasure and pain."

Hustler magazine regularly features a cartoon, "Chester the Molester." In one episode, Chester is shown in bed with three nude little girls tied up and various sexual apparatuses lying around.

Early reports from the Attorney General's Commission on Pornography found several interesting facts concerning pornography and child sexual abuse. For example, the group catalogs activities involving children, crime, and violence found in the pictures and cartoons of *Playboy, Penthouse,* and *Hustler.* They identified 2,016 child-related cartoons, of which approximately 75 percent involved children in violent or sexual acts. Many of these depict gang rape of child victims, fathers sexually abusing daughters, Santa Claus murdering a child, etc.

The Commission also said that law enforcement officers find sexually explicit materials, including these three magazines, at the scene of large numbers of sexually violent crimes. Sexually explicit materials are used to lure children into criminal sex acts perpetrated by adults.

Repeated inclusion of children in these widely distributed pornographic magazines contribute to child sexual abuse by creating perceptions of children as viable sex objects while desensitizing readers to the seriousness of child sexual abuse.

Pornography Used to Recruit
It is now common knowledge that child pornographers use pornography to recruit their victims. A 50-year-old convicted child molester, testifying before a Senate panel, offered a chilling confession of how he victimized girls for nearly 30 years.

Joseph Henry told senators he used pornographic films and photographs of children to diminish the resistance of 22 girls, ages 6 to 14, that he victimized from 1949 until he was arrested in 1978.

According to Sen. William V. Roth, Jr., R-Del., chairman of the Senate Permanent Subcommittee on Investigations, which conducted the hearing, an "inextricable connection" exists between pornography and child abuse and cannot be ignored.

Roth said: "It is chilling to realize that every photo on every page of every child pornography magazine represents the actual molestation of a child. Every photo is a permanent record of the work of a child molester. In order for child pornography to exist, a child must be exploited—and, in most cases, physically abused."

Henry said he often would show pornographic materials to the children he abused. "If a pedophile wants a little girl to do a certain act and she doesn't want to do it, he can say, 'Look, this little girl is doing it!' " he said.

Again, recall that those who profit from the sale of pornography often claim that the content of their magazines doesn't really cause readers to commit sexual crimes. Yet pornographic publishers depend on advertisers to help them make money. An advertiser is not going to spend thousands of dollars to put an ad in a pornographic magazine unless he knows the ad will cause people to act on what they read. The pornography pushers are talking out of both sides of their mouths!

Nicholas von Hoffman, a writer for the *Washington Post*, points out the discrepancy of the porn-pushers' logic. Hoffman wrote, "Why is it that some [people] believe [that] 'role models' in third-grade readers are of decisive influence on behavior when it concerns racism or male chauvinist piggery, but laugh at the assertion that pornography may also teach rape? . . . If textbooks, those vapid and insipid instruments of such slight influence, can have such sweeping effect, what are we to surmise about the effects on the impressionable young by an R- or X-rated movie, in widescreen technicolor?"

Playboy, Penthouse, and other publications would find it

difficult to exist without the endorsement and support of many advertisers such as Nissan, CBS, and RCA which endorse the publications with millions of advertising dollars. These companies tell consumers that their advertising in the magazines in no way endorses the publications. But that is not what readers would believe or what the pornographers say.

Bob Guccione, president of Penthouse, International, said in sworn testimony in a Georgia district court that an advertiser "not only buys circulation, but he buys editorial vitality and editorial credibility." He went on to say later in the testimony that "an advertiser in advertising in a publication indirectly endorses that publication."

Who Is to Blame?

A teenager on the street may live one year," estimates Franciscan Father Bruce Ritter. That's a tragedy he sees repeated over and over in his work as founder and director of the New York-based runaway shelter known as Covenant House, previously mentioned.

"A kid may live longer than that but he has been so damaged after a year he can't turn around," said Father Ritter in an interview with the *Catholic Telegraph*.

He faults not only those who market pornographic materials for the abuse and prostitution of young runaways but also an entire nation of adults who indirectly support the merchandising of young people by patronizing stores which sell pornographic magazines and by buying products promoted with sexual messages. "We reward those who use sex," he said.

Father Ritter, who works almost daily with children who have been abused, says that "the most intellectually dishonest thing a person can say is that there is no connection between pornography and sexual abuse."

A Justice Department official recommends creation of an FBI criminal-history file on child molesters. Lois Herrington, assistant attorney general, says such a file would make it possible for officials to avoid hiring child molesters as teachers, playground supervisors, or for other jobs that involve dealing with children.

Herrington said, "We have played very fast and loose with the care of our children for a long time. . . . We have no way of ascertaining . . . who is working in our schools, who is driving our school buses, or who is working as a park and recreation leader."

In most states, arrest records are confidential unless conviction results, and in child molestation cases, there are few convictions, she said. One child killer who was recently executed had 150-200 child molestation cases in his background.

Penn's Dr. Burgess offers the following advice to parents:

● *Be alert to adults who spend an undue amount of time in the company of children.* These men often prefer to spend time with children that other adults would spend with grown-ups; for example, going to a six-year-old's birthday party.

● *Be suspicious of unusual variation in a normal routine.* For instance, in one case a teacher asked that certain children come to school long before others.

● *Watch for such telling things in children as extreme anxiety around a specific adult,* declining grades, withdrawal from ordinary playmates to associate only with a certain group.

● *Pay attention to physical symptoms* such as headaches, loss of appetite or vomiting and difficulty sleeping. Genital complaints such as soreness are particularly important.

● *Be aware of a precocious sexuality in language, dress, or behavior.*

Preventive Rules for Parents

The primary rule is that parents should know where their children are at all times.

Another good practice is for parents to know the exact route their children walk to and from school and to insist that the children not take alternate routes or shortcuts through strange neighborhoods.

Parents should alert the police immediately when any suspicious activity occurs. No neighbor, friend, or relative should be shielded if guilty of sexually exploiting children. All sexual "offers" to children should be reported immediately.

Parents should play the "what if" game with children. For instance, "What if a stranger offers you a ride home?" By rehearsing possible situations, parents can help children know what to do to avoid danger.

Child molesters use their own newsletters to share techniques for seducing innocent children, according to a child advocate.

Molesters concentrate on specific age-groups, at certain times of the day, and have what they call easy steps to lure a child into sexual abuse, Kenneth Wooden told an audience in Concord, New Hampshire.

"I wish parents were as organized as child molesters and sexual abusers," said Wooden, the founder of a national computerized network for child victims. He said molesters put out national newsletters that offer such tips as using soap crayons in the bath to get young children to take off their clothes.

Children and imprisoned child molesters gave Wooden the following information that led him to some conclusions:

- Children most sought are 10–12-year-olds because they are approaching puberty and are seen by molesters as the greatest turnon.
- Most abductions take place between 3 and 6 P.M. The easy prey is a child who takes shortcuts to school, and who looks depressed or is a loner on the playground.
- The child molesters (78 percent) are white males 20-40 years old.
- Most popular car used is a two-door because it is harder to escape from, and the most popular color is blue because it more closely resembles a police car.
- While girls more often report being molested, there is a high percentage of boys who are victims but fear parental restrictions if they report it.
- The lure used most often is to ask a child for help—

directions, finding a lost puppy, or carrying books or groceries.

What Can You Do?

First, *become knowledgeable* of the subject. Dr. Shirley O'Brien's book *Child Pornography* (Kendall-Hunt Publishing Company, 1983) offers a wealth of vital information on the problem.

Second, *report child-sexual abuse* if you know about it. Sexual molestation, child pornography, and child prostitution are crimes. Instances should definitely be reported. This can be done anonymously if so desired. Where possible, a full information report is preferable. If you give your name, address, and phone number, your report has more credibility. Also, it may be that authorities would need this information in order to contact you later.

Third, *support stricter legislation and prosecution* of sex offenses against children.

Fourth, *refuse to shop in stores that sell pornographic magazines*. Be sure to inform the stores why you are ceasing to do business with them. Encourage others to do the same. Pornography contributes to the problem. Pornography is directly linked to child sexual abuse.

In summary, the answer to the problem of sexual exploitation of children is a shared one. Individual and cooperative action will be needed to seek short- and long-range solutions. Not all will agree as to the right path to follow in the eradication of this cancer. Regardless of the path taken or the action chosen, the important thing is the depth of commitment of those who are engaged in the battle. One thing that would be helpful to all concerned is for those of us who care to join hands in this simple affirmation: "I am only one. I cannot do everything. But I can do *something*. What I can do, I ought to do. And what I ought to do, by the grace of God *I will do.*"

5.
A Pediatrician's View of Pornography

By Dr. Elizabeth Holland,
Memphis Pediatrician

What I have to say is not to shock you, though perhaps this might well happen. What I have to say is not to offend your sensibilities—though again, I recognize that this may take place. I simply want to share with you a few of my experiences over the past ten years in treating victims of pornographers. Of treating the children who have been affected, who have been abused, who have been damaged for life by those who feed on pornography.

There exist in our nation and in our area and in our community those men and women who have been abused, who have been damaged for life by those who feed on pornography. There exist in our nation and in our area and in our community those men and women who have a sickness, who feed on dirty pictures and pornography. And when touching pictures and fantasizing and looking no longer satisfies these people's insatiable appetite, then they move. And they move to live children. I know— because I treat these children.

Recently there came into my office a distraught mother with a 14-year-old son, a 12-year-old daughter, an 11-year-old daughter, and an 8-year-old son. As her story unfolded, it appeared that her 14-year-old son had been purchasing pornographic magazines and reading them in his bedroom; after reading them and arousing himself sexually to the point that he could no longer contain himself, he would go into the bedrooms of his 12-year-old sister, of his 11-year-old sister, and of his 8-year-old brother and rape them—several times weekly. It further unfolded that this had continued for five years. If you can subtract with me, the 14-year-old boy was nine when he began his activities. His 12-year-old sister was seven. His 11-year-old sister was six and his 8-year-old brother was three years old when he began to be raped by his 9-year-old brother who fed on pornography and graduated to live children!

I treated a young boy in my office who was four years old. His family was divorced. He lived with his mother. He visited his father on weekends. From the time he was two, when the child would return home to his mother after visiting his father, he would cry and be irritable—and none of us could figure out why. At age four we learned that the father of this two-year-old boy had been systematically raping this child in his home—many times, every weekend, for two years. The father fed on pornographic magazines. He shared them with his two-year-old child and then forced his two-year-old child into anal intercourse. Immediately following one visit with his father, I examined this child. His rectum looked like hamburger meat.

I have been told by many children who have been there—I have never seen this house—but I have been told that there is a house in Memphis where children are photographed in various sexual poses with each other, with adults, with men, with women, with animals. They are photographed and the pictures are distributed to various kiddie pornographic magazines. And yet, do you know what I hear when I speak out against pornography? When I stand and tell these stories to people who are not concerned? Do you know what I hear? I hear from them that I don't have the right to determine what other people watch in their living rooms. I wouldn't subscribe to the Playboy channel, but what right do I have to say that someone who is willing to pay the money can't subscribe? I don't have the right to prevent this from being offered in the Memphis area. I don't have the right to prevent you from watching it if you'd like—yet I look at the children who have been abused and who have been beaten and who have been battered by those who feed on this pornography. I say that I not only have the right to prevent this pornography from spreading in this community, I have a moral obligation.

Let me paraphrase for you a story that you're all very likely familiar with—Ezekiel, chapter 3. The Lord is calling Ezekiel. He says, "Oh, son of man, I have made you a watchman of the house of Israel. I send you to the house of Israel with My warning. You must go to them and you must warn them of their wicked ways. If you refuse to and the wicked man dies in his sins, then I will hold you to blame and his blood is on your hands. If you go and warn him and he refuses to listen, he will die in his sins but you are blameless. And if you go and warn him and he listens, and he repents, then he will come unto life and you have saved your soul" (3:17-19). Do I have the right to speak out against evil that exists in this world and in my community and in my neighborhood? As God said to Ezekiel, I must go and you must go. If we refuse to go, those of us who have been spoken to and commanded by the Lord, if we refuse to go, the blood of these innocent children is on our hands.

Not long ago police brought a little four-year-old girl into my office. She had a torn and lacerated vagina. It seems that her father, her uncle, and her brothers would buy pornographic literature and would pass it around among themselves, and laugh and tell dirty jokes—and finally, when they were tired of reading and tired of fantasizing, they would take this four-year-old child and they would all rape her. The child had been taken to another doctor, one year previously, for the same problem. This doctor had chosen to ignore the signs and the symptoms; he prescribed ointment; and sent a three-year-old girl back into this situation for another year of torture and fear and pain. Now who's to blame? The family? Yes. But what about the doctor who knew? What about the one who understood and refused to act because he did not want to get involved? I submit that his guilt is as great or greater than those who actually perpetrated this violence on that innocent child.

I once treated two young girls, ages 9 and 11, whose father purchased sadistic pornographic literature. One afternoon he took the mother and the two daughters onto his front porch with a pile of sadistic pornographic literature, and he required that they all share in and look at it. And then he took a gun and he held it to the mother's head and proceeded to rape her unmercifully in front of his two daughters. And when he had finished raping her, he calmly pulled the trigger and killed her in front of his daughters. Then he held the gun to their heads and he raped them in the same manner and said, "I will kill you in the same manner if you tell anyone what I have done." I treated these children for two years before I could get one word out of either. They had lived in abject terror because of what they had seen and what they had experienced.

I treated a three-year-old who visited his mother on weekends. One day, during a check-up after such a visit, I noticed he had large, draining sores on his penis. He had been sexually abused by the mother. The child had venereal disease. The venereal disease we can treat. The scars from the experience we cannot treat.

Don't tell me I don't have the right—and don't tell me that you don't have the right—or the obligation—to speak out against the criminal spread of pornography in our midst.

Another thing I hear is, "It'll never work. There are too many of them; there are too few of us. They're too big. There's too much money involved. Keep up the good work, brother; I agree with what you're doing but you're fighting a losing battle. I mean, why should I turn in my converter? I enjoy my TV. It's not going to work. They'll never remove *Playboy;* they'll never refuse to offer it. Why should I deprive myself of the shows I enjoy? You're fighting a losing battle. Count me out."

Once again, let me paraphrase for you a story that you all know. We'll go to the twelfth chapter of Acts. Peter and James had been preaching in the streets. Herod had had James killed with a sword. Peter had been thrown into prison and he was chained between two guards in a dark dungeon. And in the middle of the night the angel of the Lord appeared to Peter and he said, "Stand up." And Peter stood up. And when Peter stood up the chains fell off. And then the angel said, "Put on your clothes. Put on your shoes. Put on your coat, and follow me." Peter did, following the angel out of the dungeon, out to the iron gate which had no key; and the iron gate opened to them of its own accord. Notice in this story that God did not do one thing for Peter that night that Peter could do for himself. God could have picked up Peter from that dungeon and translated him to the home of Mary, the mother of John Mark, where the church had gathered and was praying for his release. God could have done that. But He didn't. He said, "Stand up." And Peter obeyed. And then the chains fell off.

You know, I can almost hear old Peter in that dungeon, if he had been infected with the defeated attitude that prevails among many Christians today. When the angel appeared and said, "Stand up," I can hear him saying, "Oh, no. I mean, these chains are heavy and I might wake up those guards on either side. There are two of them and there is only one of me. And actually, I've gotten fairly comfortable down here.

"Now, angel, I don't think you've thought this through very carefully. I mean, we have to go through this whole jail and there are guards everywhere. We have to crawl up those creaky steps—man, have you heard those steps creak? And once we get out, don't forget that big iron gate out there. There's no way! There's no key. We can't climb that gate! No, I think I'd rather stay here. Maybe they'll let me live. Maybe they'll just flog me and let me go. No, I don't think I'll go with you—but thank you. Thanks for trying. Thanks for thinking about me."

No. Peter stood up and the chains fell off. And the angel said, "Come. Put on your clothes. Follow me. Put on your coat." Peter followed that angel and he obeyed the Lord and when he reached the impossible iron gate, the iron gate opened to him of its own accord. You see, God's call on my life and God's call on your life is to do the things that are possible and to trust Him with the things that are impossible.

I am outraged when I am told that I do not have the right to speak out against pornography in our community. I am outraged when I am told that it's a battle we cannot win and therefore we must not try. I am outraged when I put my hands in the wounds of abused, battered children, the victims of people who have fed on pornographers' filth. I am outraged when I sit and hold a beautiful young girl on my lap and she wraps her arms around my neck and cries, "Why? Why did he hurt me?" I have no answer for her except that good men and good women and good ministers sat back and did nothing.

I treated a family who were brought in by the police. There were a mother and father in their middle twenties. There were a four-year-old boy and a three-year-old girl. It seems that the mother and father were producers of kiddie porn, and they had used their children for two years as models. The children were required to strip naked and engage in sexual acts with each other, and to engage in sexual acts with adults and animals. People buy photographs of this filth. There's a market for this. It's a multi-million-dollar business in our nation today. And because of this these children have suffered untold harm.

Now who do you think bears the responsibility for these children? The mother and father who photographed? Yes. They are their responsibility. What about the distributors of kiddie porn who take this material and distribute it? What about those who buy it and feed on it and create the market? I would say to you that they're all responsible. But I would also say to you that those of us in this room and myself are responsible if we refuse to become involved in the fight against this filth.

God calls us to do the possible. He'll take care of the impossible. What's possible to us? I would say to you that there is one thing that is possible to all of us, and I would earnestly enlist your support in fervent, groaning prayer before the Lord God Almighty. We need to fall on our faces and say, "God, we have sinned in what we have done and what we have failed to do." James tells us that the "effectual, fervent prayer of a righteous man availeth much," and when we reach out, God will answer us. We must reach out and claim His promises. God has said, "If My people . . . will humble themselves and pray, if they will seek My face, and if they will turn from their wicked ways, then I, I the Lord will hear their prayer in heaven, and I will forgive their sins and I will heal their land" (paraphrased from 2 Chronicles 7:14).

This is our possibility, friends. We have to reach out and touch and claim the power of Almighty God for the cleansing and the healing of our land. You see, I'm a doctor. I can suture lacerations, I can put Band-Aids on wounds, I can put ointments, I can give antibiotics. But I cannot heal the damage that has been done to these children who have been abused by those who feed on pornography. I cannot erase the hurt and the bewilderment and the fear from the eyes of those who have been affected by pornography as it exists today. And yet, the purveyors of pornography want to bring it into my living room and into your living room and into the living room of anyone who wants to plunk down a few dollars and feed on sickness and disease and decay. I can't treat the effects—I can't treat these children who have been abused. The damage is done.

I'm reminded of the disease of polio, which we fought for so many years. I can't treat the effects of polio—but polio has effectively been conquered in our nation. How? Through a vaccine, and we now prevent it. Polio can be treated by prevention—not by treatment of its effects. Pornography? I cannot treat the effects of the pornographers on children. They will wear these handicaps for the rest of their lives. But pornography can be prevented. It can be prevented, it can be conquered, and it can be stopped if we can enlist the help of good people throughout this land who are willing to stand up and be counted in this effort. Please, please, join us and help stop the spread of this filth in our land. Please, help us protect the innocent children. Please.

6.
The Victims of "Victimless" Pornography

Have you ever been told that pornography is a "victimless" crime? Nothing could be further from the truth. Both those who use pornography and those who suffer at the hands of those who use pornography are victims.

Bill Smith and John Ferguson are two victims who used pornography. The children they abused are also victims. Smith and Ferguson (not their real names) became addicted to pornography. It gained a grip so strong that the two men now view their last pornographic magazine like an alcoholic views his last drink.

They can tell you about the magazines, the books, and the videotapes that comprise the $7 billion pornography business. They can tell you about the allure of pornography, a grip that became more viselike with each stop at pornographic bookstores and theaters. They can tell you how this unquenchable desire for perverted materials eventually cost them their freedom. They are convicted sex offenders.

Smith and Ferguson testified before the U.S. Senate Subcommittee on Juvenile Justice in Pittsburgh.

"I see pornography itself as a catalyst to the fantasies of a sex offender," said Smith.

Ferguson added, "There's no doubt it was a contributing factor to my problems. It gives you ideas. It gets your mind stimulated, your head going, your body going, and your fantasies going. . . . Pornography OK's the act."

Explaining his sexual abuse of girls as young as 11, Ferguson said, "The only way I could find gratification was to victimize someone younger, weaker, and less knowledgeable."

A victimless crime? In Dane County, Wisconsin an attorney died in what investigators called a sexual bondage escapade. At the scene of death they found pornographic magazines, homosexual films, and signs of sadomasochistic services. The man died after being tied and suspended from the ceiling.

Isolated cases? Not by any means. One thing the pornographers do not want the public to know about is that there are victims of pornography.

A 30-year-old man suspected in 25 or more Austin, Texas rapes apparently took pictures of his victims during the attacks. When officers went to his home, they found his car parked on the street. On the passenger seat were a pornographic magazine, a Polaroid camera, and a nude photograph of one of his victims. But still many insist that pornography is a victimless crime.

Cable TV Instructs 15-year-old

Pornography encourages harmful behavior on the part of otherwise innocent people. A reader recently sent me a copy of an Ann Landers letter from a desperate 15-year-old boy. He explained that his 12-year-old girlfriend claims she is pregnant.

The boy then wrote, "Can this really be? We only had sex once. Can a girl get pregnant the first time? We were just seeing what it was like after watching a movie on cable TV. We are too young to be parents, aren't we? Please hurry your answer. I need to know if it's possible and what to do."

The networks and pornographers still tell you that their sex-oriented and pornographic movies or television programs do not affect anyone or cause them to imitate what they see. One must wonder how long we will continue to buy that big lie. Of course they never tell advertisers that seeing or hearing their products advertised will not cause people to buy them. They tell them exactly the opposite.

Pornography is again and again seen as the motivator for sexual abuse. "Nobody knows the trouble I've seen, nobody knows but Jesus," began a recent letter. The writer said that as a child she had been the victim of sex abuse by adults who indulged in pornography. She is now determined to protect her own daughters and to guide them in the truth of the Lord.

This concerned mother made one other very important point in her letter. She wrote that her older daughter had recently observed that most adults would complain if a truckload of rapists, murderers, and child molesters were shipped into town. Yet sophisticated, liberal, even supposedly Christian people look the other way when pornography shops operate, pornographic magazines are sold in a local store, and X-rated movies are shown on local theater screens.

Is pornography a victimless crime? Lt. Darrell Pope, head of the Michigan State Police investigative research unit, told a group the following story.

"A 19-year-old girl just off from work was walking down the street. A 19-year-old man pulls up in his car. She knows him and he says to her, 'Do you want a ride home?' She accepts

"Instead of taking her home, he drove her out into the country and demanded her services. She refused. He had been reading pornographic magazines. In fact, found in his car were a number of pornographic magazines depicting piquerism. Piquerism is piercing or stabbing of a person.

"When he finally finished with that body, the young woman had been sexually assaulted by every means possible and, ladies and gentlemen, she had been stabbed 57 times."

Lieutenant Pope closed with this question: "Does pornography contribute to such an assault? You be the judge," he said.

Pope reports that during the years 1956-79 there were about 38,000 reported sexual assault cases in his state. In 41 percent of the cases, pornography was used just prior to or during the crime. That means that in Michigan alone 14,580 victims were attacked as a direct result of their attackers "acting out" sexual impulses generated from viewing pornography.

Pornography takes its tragic victims in many ways as it invades every segment of our society. For example, a New York town in midsummer was shocked by news that the local elementary school principal was arrested on federal charges of mailing obscene material. The material reportedly included pictures of child pornography.

The story is further evidence that none of us should assume we are not affected by pornography. Its pervasiveness is a danger to the survival of our nation and the institutions that have made it great. The church, the family, the education system—all are threatened and affected by the very presence of pornography.

A Bad Actor!

People act out the scenes they view in pornographic magazines and films. In the state of Washington, Clark County sheriff's deputies charged Clark Hazen in the murder of Shirley Russell, 65, and his daughter, Donna Russell, 27. Authorities said the two were found in a trailer, each body having a bullet wound in the head. According to the authorities, Hazen had rented two pornographic videotapes. Deputies who later confiscated the videotapes said Clark Hazen returned the tapes without rewinding them. One of the tapes was stopped just after a scene depicting a woman in a position similar to that in which Donna Russell's body was found.

Harold Koput told a psychiatrist he took pleasure in seeing the star of a late-night cable TV movie slash a woman to death and rape her. Following the movie, Koput went out to reenact in real life what he had seen on TV. Taking his cue from the movie, he went in search of a woman to be his sex slave. "I wanted to do what they did on Channel 24," he told the psychiatrist.

His victim was Lucille Nelson, whom he had met in a bar that night. Her bludgeoned body was found the next day in a snowbank. She had been hit in the head 12 times with a tire iron and stabbed three times each in the neck and abdomen.

Koput was convicted of first-degree murder in the case. Bruce Lowe, the lead prosecuting attorney, condemned the pay TV station's films, saying the movies serve only to trigger the sick into violent behavior.

Lowe said of the convicted Koput, "The smut he viewed on television only stimulated his perversion."

A seven-year-old boy in St. Petersburg, Florida testified that he and his nine-year-old brother were imitating actions they had seen in their mother's sex magazines when they assaulted an eight-month-old girl who died of the attack.

The testimony stated that the sexual abuse of the infant, with objects the boys picked up in the bedroom, was mimicry of acts seen in hard-core sex books their mother kept around the house. The mother acknowledged she kept pornographic magazines and that the boys could have had access to them.

Tom McCoun, representing the nine-year-old, told the juvenile judge the younger boy testified that he and his brother, in sexually assaulting the infant with a pencil and coat hanger, were mimicking what they had seen in the sex books.

The infant, who suffered Down's Syndrome and had a defective heart, was found on the floor in a bedroom where the two young boys were sleeping. She died shortly afterward. Medical Examiner Joan Wood testified that the cause of death was "blunt trauma" to the chest and abdomen. She said it was consistent with one of the boys kneeling on the baby.

Pornography affects not only minds already perverted, but it can pervert minds. Someone sent us newspaper articles of one of the most tragic and brutal incidents we have read about. The rape and attempted murder of a 17-year-old high school student rocked the little town of Joyce, Washington. David Eugene Pyles, a 29-year-old Army veteran with an enviable family background and an impeccable record, was convicted of first-degree rape and attempted first-degree murder.

Pyles was discovered to be a connoisseur of pornographic movies, particularly those of the violent sex variety. Investigating officers also found among his effects: a scrapbook of nude magazine photos; a journal (thought to have been written by Pyles) describing brutal sexual acts and torture; and portions of sexually explicit novels stapled together, describing brutal sexual acts.

What kind of man was David Eugene Pyles? As mentioned, he

had virtually a spotless past. He had served in the U.S. Army in Iran and Germany. His parents are the epitome of high moral standards.

Upon his release from the Army in 1982, Pyles returned home; and another side to Pyles became evident—a side that few people had seen or even had cause to suspect. The tragic events of October 13, 14, and 15, 1982 apparently took the following sequence:

On October 13 about 11 A.M., Pyles drove his company vehicle to a Port Angeles video store and rented two films. One was *Blood Tide,* about a monster that kills a virgin once a year. The other was *Unseen,* about a mentally retarded man locked in the basement of a motel. The man escapes occasionally and kills women staying in the motel.

About 3 P.M. the same day, Pyles went to Fort Watson Video, where he rented *Eaten Alive,* which is about alligators that eat people; and *Blue Beard,* about a rich man who marries beautiful women, then kills them and freezes them in a vault.

Such was the diet of perversion with which Pyles fed his mind. A coworker who shared a motel room with Pyles later testified that Pyles had viewed *Blue Beard* the morning the girl was attacked.

On October 14 about 1 P.M., a teenage girl decided to take a walk. As she strolled along the roadside, she was run down by a car driven by Pyles.

Pyles stopped, and at knife point, forced her into the car and took her to an isolated area where he raped her, then stabbed her, and cut her throat. Only when the girl pretended to be dead did her assailant return to his car.

He sat in his car for a few minutes, returning several times to the ravine where he had thrown her. On his final trip, he picked up a rock and struck her on the head, then returned to his car and drove away.

The girl heard an approaching car, and though severely wounded, managed to get up the bank to the road. A 16-year-old boy stopped and took the injured girl to a nearby home for help. The neighbor who took her in recalled the girl "was naked and she was just covered with blood. She had blonde hair and it was just dripping with blood."

Late that night, after getting descriptions of the attacker and his vehicle, police arrested Pyles in his motel room.

On October 15 investigators found the following in Pyles' flight-type bag: a manila envelope with 32 pages of notebook paper containing nude magazine photos glued to them in scrapbook fashion; a journal including many pages describing brutal sexual acts and torture; and portions of sexually explicit novels torn from books and stapled together, describing brutal sexual acts.

During the trial, Sheriff's Inspector Fred DeFrang told the court that handwritten notebooks and films found among Pyles' possessions "depicted various ways of torturing women, restraining women, and killing women."

He said weapons described in the journals were "cutting and puncturing devices—knives and weapons which would puncture the flesh." A two-hour film in his possession appeared to be a compilation of the most brutal portions of other movies.

Thus David Eugene Pyles fed his mind on perversion and proceeded very methodically to perpetrate that perversion upon an innocent young girl.

These and thousands upon thousands of other people are the victims of pornography. The big lie is that pornography is a victimless crime.

It astounds me to hear people still use the phrase "victimless crime" in relationship to pornography. Very clearly, we are *all* victims.

7.
The Media View of Pornography

How does the national, secular media deal with pornography and those who oppose it?

One episode of CBS's *Simon and Simon* is typical. It portrayed a Christian as a triple-X-rated theater manager. The plot involved a young woman who was displayed on a poster advertising a pornographic movie. She hired Simon and Simon to find the film's distributor. She was under 18 when she posed nude for some film footage which was later spliced into the pornographic film. She protested that she never posed in any sexual acts. *At no time in the TV program are negative comments made on pornography.* The only issue was that the main character was not of legal age at the time of filming.

The first step in finding the distributor was to find the theater manager. As the Simon brothers approach the ticket booth of the XXX-rated theater, the woman inside said to someone on the phone, "Tell her we're going to be a little late for choir practice, Harry."

Identified as a "Christian" character by this comment, this grandmotherly woman turns out to be the theater manager. Not only does she promote pornography, saying, "Fred Astaire movies don't sell tickets anymore, Sonny," she and her husband view it regularly, previewing the films for her theater.

A pattern of such negative, hypocritical "Christian" characters exists on network programming.

Broadcasting magazine headlined it "Another Victory for the First" when U.S. District Judge William Hoeveler struck down a Miami, Florida city ordinance regulating indecent material on cable TV. The reference was to the First Amendment. The National Cable Television Association was quick to praise the court's decision. NCTA president Thomas Wheeler said, "The court has distinguished cable from broadcast television and aligned it with the print media."

What this means to the viewing public—if the judge's ruling is allowed to stand—is that cable TV programming evidently will have no restrictions. The televisions in our dens will soon include the same explicit pornography which *Hustler, Penthouse,* and *Playboy* have been marketing for a long time and which currently is shown in the X-rated movie houses.

Hoeveler struck down a law which was approved by a majority of citizens in Miami who did not want cable pornography in their city. Hoeveler, in his ruling, indicated that the rights of a handful of pornographers outweighed the rights of the majority of citizens in Miami.

Newsweek Reporting Unbiased?

"The War Against Pornography" was *Newsweek* magazine's cover story in a special issue dealing with pornography dated March 18, 1985. *Newsweek* writers composed one lengthy feature and several companion articles. The tone and conclusion of the article lead the reader to question *Newsweek*'s objectivity in the matter. The major conclusion, which addresses First Amendment rights, is in direct conflict with the reality of law as defined by the Supreme Court.

Newsweek put down the antipornography forces when the article concluded: "The crusaders' zeal clearly poses a threat to First Amendment freedoms."

According to the Supreme Court, however, the First Amendment has *never* protected obscenity. A 1973 decision in *Miller vs. California* held that a work can be banned if it is patently offensive to "contemporary community standards."

Thus *Newsweek* accused those who fight pornography of endangering a "freedom" that never existed.

The editorial bias of *Newsweek* also surfaced in a summary of the *Newsweek* poll. In one section of the poll, respondents were asked if laws should totally ban such things as nude magazines, magazines showing adult sexual relations, magazines showing sexual violence, X-rated theaters, X-rated video cassettes, etc.

In each category clear majorities favored either a total ban or no public display, although clear majorities did not always fall into the ban category. The average percentage of persons who favored no restriction on pornography was in reality quite low—just above 16 percent.

Acting on this information, *Newsweek* felt it fair to conclude: "The poll also makes perfectly clear the acceptance of porn in American life: clear majorities favored the continued sale of X-rated movies and sexually explicit magazines. . . ."

The subtle bias is carefully couched in such positive terms as "acceptance," "favored," and "clear majorities."

Another interesting fact is that the article never considered pornography as a moral issue. It spoke glibly about how pornography degrades women, about the rapidly increasing sexual violence in pornography, about rape and abuse related to pornography.

Yet pornography was never addressed as a moral issue. Nowhere in the five-page article was there a hint that filming of normal and perverted ultimate sex acts is a moral issue. Nowhere in the article was there a suggestion that bondage, sadomasochistic torture, and bestiality films are morally depraved and unfit for release in our society.

When speaking of pornography defenders, *Newsweek* described one pornography star as being from a Mormon family. One of the hallmarks of Mormonism, of course, is strong commitment to family values. Another pornography defender *Newsweek* quoted is Al Goldstein, publisher of one of the nation's most vile pornographic magazines titled *Screw*. Goldstein is called a "legal scholar."

Newsweek, on the other hand, described antipornography leaders with repeated use of such slanted terms as "radical feminists," "right-wing fundamentalists," "itinerant law professor," and "radical New York writer." According to the article, only a "scattering of psychologists" support the opposition's contention that pornography is harmful to society.

Newsweek cited two psychologist-researchers, both of whom stopped short of indicting pornography for the sharp rise in sexual abuse in the country. The article did *not,* however, note such studies as that by psychologist Victor Cline at the University of Utah, who finds that viewing pornography increases the likelihood of a man's committing rape.

Neither does *Newsweek* seem to know of the study by University of New Hampshire researchers Dr. Murray Straus and Dr. Larry Baron, who found that the states with the highest per capita sales of pornographic magazines also have the highest rape rates.

Individuals opposing pornography included three feminists, a councilwoman, a civic leader, and a pornography victim. Quotes from this side amounted to some 20 lines of copy.

In some 50 lines of copy, individuals from the propornography side were quoted. I learned from a reliable source that *Newsweek*'s list of propornography figures amounts to nothing less than a who's who in the pornography world. Included were six pornography producers and distributors; two pornography actresses; two ACLU lawyers; a Playboy lawyer; a Los Angeles lawyer with a well-known track record for defending pornographers; one feminist; and the late Kenneth Tynan, who wrote "In Praise of Hard Core," described by *Newsweek* reporter Peter McGrath as a "courageous attempt at a head-on defense of pornography." McGrath also referred to the triple-X movie *Misty Beethoven* as "graphic sexual depiction, but still, good, clean fun."

Whatever the purpose of the article, it was in effect an open forum for propornography voices all the way from the ACLU to pornographic actors who copulate before cameras and call it art.

Ex-FBI Agent Bill Kelly, responded to the *Newsweek* article with these words: "I failed to see any representation in *Newsweek* of the organized crime influence in the pornography world. In my experience, I can tell you that the pornography /obscenity business is a high-gross, low-risk industry which is, to a large extent, taken over and controlled by traditional organized crime elements, including several leading Mafia families and also by other organized groups not directly controlled by Mafia elements."

But *Newsweek*, of course, did not tell their readers about that.

60 Minutes Coverage Also Slanted

The CBS *60 Minutes* feature "The Politics of Porn" told of the battle in Minneapolis to get an ordinance enacted which would make dealing in pornography a civil offense, defining it as sexual abuse against women.

The segment was at best unbalanced and incomplete. First, producer Joel Bernstein carefully selected attractive, calm, professional people to interview in opposition to the emotional Andrea Dworkin, who helped draft the ordinance along with law professor Catharine MacKinnon. Second, it treated the issue of pornography as if it were *only* a feminist issue. Third, the feature was another example of how the careful choice of words (always "censorship," never "control," etc.) is used by the networks to move a story in a particular direction. Fourth, some might even contend that the segment included unnecessary pornographic scenes for the purpose of titillation.

60 Minutes reporter Ed Bradley conducted the interviews and narrated the segment, leading off with the questions, "Should anyone be allowed to stop a bookstore from selling pornographic magazines or novels? Or stop a movie house from showing a pornographic film?" The camera quickly moved into a pornography shop to pan across the tiers of pornographic magazines with nude bodies on their perverse covers.

Dworkin and MacKinnon were employed by the city of Minneapolis to draft the ordinance which stirred local controversy and gained national notoriety. Their proposal was adopted by the city council but vetoed by the mayor. Bradley first interviewed the two women, then throughout the segment Dworkin was reintroduced several times. Dworkin was not well-dressed by "professional" standards as her opponents were. She was also portrayed by CBS as an emotional, perhaps even reactionary, woman. She stood alone as the authority *for* the ordinance in contrast to an array of attractive, well-dressed professional people whom Bradley used to oppose the ordinance. (The ordinance's co-author, Professor MacKinnon, was afforded minimal camera time.)

In his choice of "experts" to refute the feminists, producer Bernstein stacked the deck with this impressive list: a university sex therapist who uses pornography in her therapy sessions and who testifies for pay on behalf of pornography dealers all over the country; two legitimate social science researchers who disdain the very mention of the word censorship; an American Civil Liberties Union attorney who apparently shudders at the thought of any kind of restriction on pornography; and a Minneapolis pornography dealer.

To poll the opposition, the camera came first to ACLU attorney Matthew Stark, executive director of Minnesota CLU, as he denounced Dworkin and MacKinnon, saying, "The MacKinnon censorship ordinance, as I publicly stated, is a piece of trash! . . . Of course, women are denigrated in books and magazines. There's no argument about that. The question is, 'What do you do about it?' We say one of the first things you *don't* do is ban the sale of books in this city."

The second blow for the opposition came from the CBS treatment of Bradley's interview with Drs. Neil Malamuth (UCLA) and Edward Donnerstein (University of Wisconsin), social science researchers especially known for their work in the area of pornography. In narration dubbed in after the interview, Bradley claimed, "They say there is no evidence that aggressive pornography causes violence against women . . ," but the researchers had no opportunity to respond to the statement.

The truth is, Malamuth and Donnerstein's work (cited in chapter 3) has a marked negative effect on males, even leading men to increased possibility of themselves raping someone.

Bradley asked if it is not "normal" for young boys to sneak a look at pornographic material as they become curious about sex. Donnerstein replied yes, but pointed out that 15 years ago, they probably would have seen—at most—pictures of nude women in *Playboy*. He then raised the question of what a boy today will find: " . . . given the new technology—home video, HBO, the proliferation of incredible amounts of violence—perhaps the first thing he's going to be introduced to which has anything to do with contact, in a sexual nature, with women is a violent rape, it's the degradation of women, it's the mutilation of women. Is that going to have an effect? I think it does."

Bradley then seized the opportunity to capitalize on the researchers' reluctance to endorse the antipornography ordinance. Anticipating the negative response, he asked, "So what's the answer. Is it censorship?"

"No! Not at all," quickly responded Donnerstein.

Malamuth added, "We're in the wrong position, I think, to suggest the answer. That's not our role. Our role is to be objective as scientists."

A fourth witness for the opposition was Joel Shinder, whose family has operated a Minneapolis bookstore for some 70 years. Shinder was never called a pornography dealer, but was portrayed as a legitimate businessman who "sells everything from intellectual magazines to hard-core pornography."

Bradley's leading question to Shinder was, "You see censorship involved in this, then?"

"Absolutely!" was Shinder's reply.

Most interesting was Bradley's stroll through Shinder's bookstore. The two men quite obviously avoided the hard-core section and headed straight for a section of paperback novels, most featuring covers with couples in suggestive or explicit sexual illustrations. Asked Bradley, "Is this the kind of book that would be called 'sexually explicit'?"

Shinder replied, "They're designed to allow fantasies to play their part in a woman's life."

Despite Shinder's identifying the novels with female readers, Bradley continued, "Who buys this kind of stuff?"

Shinder: "Women."

Bradley responded as if he were shocked, "Women?"

Probably the most striking of the propornography team was University of Minnesota sex therapist Dr. Sharon Satterfield, head of the Human Sexuality Program. Bradley introduced Satterfield by explaining that she uses pornography in sex therapy and in treatment she offers sex offenders.

Again, knowing the attitude of his subject and seeking a predictable response, Bradley said that "men might see it (pornography) and go out and abuse women."

Satterfield, a poised, attractive woman, replied with soft-voiced authority, "The only kind of person that we find might do that is someone who has trouble distinguishing between fantasy and reality. . . . It's a little frightening to a professional who works in this field to see this kind of ordinance . . . ."

Bradley, true to form, registered total dismay and shock at the doctor's astonishing revelation that even the Bible might be banned under the MacKinnon ordinance.

One detail CBS omitted about Dr. Satterfield is her reputation for traveling across the country to testify on behalf of pornographers who have been brought to court. Dr. Satterfield is compensated for her time and efforts. According to law officials in Fort Lauderdale, Dr. Satterfield was there to testify as an expert witness for pornographer-defendants in the celebrated MIPORN (Miami pornography) case. Twelve of the nation's top pornographers had been convicted in the operation, and 14 more were awaiting trial. Pornographers Larry Nelson and Roland Boudreault, owners of a San Francisco pornography distributorship, were convicted on three counts of interstate transportation of obscene materials. The convictions came about as a result of the FBI's undercover operation MIPORN, and represents the only such far-reaching federal obscenity investigation in recent memory.

Dr. Satterfield was there on behalf of the pornographers. She testified to the serious scientific content of a film with a pornographic title unsuitable for these pages. For her testimony, she reportedly was paid a fee of $2,000-$2,500.

In the transcript of the trial (U.S vs. Boudreault and Nelson) is found the following exchange between Dr. Satterfield and Prosecuting Attorney Marcella Cohen:

COHEN: Isn't it true that in one of the films that they show at your school, one of the films depicts a nun being raped. Isn't that true?

SATTERFIELD: The film depicts the fantasy of a nun. This is a classic film. . . .

COHEN: I am asking if the film depicts a nun being raped.

SATTERFIELD: Yes.

COHEN: And does that film have serious scientific value?

SATTERFIELD: Yes, it does.

So there they are, the CBS gallery of professional "free speech" advocates—the articulate ACLU attorney Stark; the detached, scientific researchers Malamuth and Donnerstein; the local businessman fearing loss of income; and the attractive sex therapist Satterfield—all measured against the flamboyant, emotional Andrea Dworkin. Two of them depend on pornography for at least a part of their livelihood. It becomes quite clear what CBS thought of the Dworkin-MacKinnon ordinance.

That CBS considered it only a feminist issue is also quite evident. In the coverage of a community meeting at which local residents addressed the issue, the only proponents were two outspoken feminists. But opposing the ordinance at that meeting was one woman who said that she had been raped twice and that both times it had more to do with alcohol than anything else. The other "random" speaker against the proposal was a mother who, holding her small child, spoke of her fear of this abridgement of free speech and who called the ordinance "Orwellian." Strangely absent from the CBS roster of debaters (both for and against) was any voice which spoke of the issue from a moral perspective.

Another way in which the segment was slanted was through Bradley's choice of words, which helped CBS accomplish its apparent goal to be perceived as a champion of freedom. For example, the segment leaned heavily on the word *censorship* when referring to the ordinance. Those who opposed it, on the other hand, were advocates of "free speech." And Joel Shinder was a bookstore owner, a businessman, not a seller of pornography.

As to the pornography clips themselves, CBS began with scenes from a movie of sexual violence. Numerous scenes panned over the rows and rows of pornographic magazines, their covers visible with graphic female nudity and couples photographed in sexual contact. Another part of the feature carried a brief portion of a pornographic film with a woman bathing. Dr. Donnerstein narrated the film clips of a psychotic killer entering the house and using a gun to drive nails into the woman's body in a chase about the house.

The inclusion of the explicit scenes might be considered in light of an analysis of television by Dr. David L. McKenna. Dr. McKenna wrote in the March/April 1984 issue of *United Evangelical Action,* "The process television uses to move into forbidden subjects is seductively alluring. First, intrigue broaches the subject by using double meanings that let the imagination of the viewer supply the image, color, and details for the act. Second, information, flat and factual, is presented for discussion of the subject under the guise of a public service contribution. Third, the subject is dramatized with all the exposure and emotions that test the limits of the television code.

"Finally, then the subject is saturated. Media overkill produces either boredom with the subject or acceptance of it as another part of sexual freedom. . . .

CBS handled "The Politics of Pornography" with predictable network mentality, subtly implying a belief that freedom requires no restrictions on any aspect of life—even on the $7 billion pornographic industry which daily destroys untold lives, both physically and morally.

Not reported in "The Politics of Pornography" by CBS was the fact that CBS, which was already distributing Playboy's pornographic video cassettes, also owns 50 percent of Cablevision's Rainbow Programming Service. Rainbow is the company which distributes the pornographic Playboy Channel. CBS has a financial interest in making sure that pornography is handled with kid gloves.

This attitude of CBS toward pornography isn't confined to news reporting. It is also in the network's entertainment programming. CBS slipped in a quick endorsement for pornography at the beginning of one episode of *Kate and Allie*.

The episode's introduction, which bears no relevance to the show's storyline, features Kate and Allie walking by a sidewalk newsstand.

"Oh, it's disgusting!" declares Allie, picking up a paper and paying the vendor. "You can't even buy a newspaper around here without being assaulted by all those smutty magazines!"

"Well, don't look," responds Kate as the two women pause to wander around the newsstand gazing at the pornographic magazines they pretend to disdain.

"How can you help but look? They're all over the place," insists Allie.

"That's the price you pay for living in a free country," reasons Kate.

"That's not freedom. That's moral anarchy!" Allie responds.

"You want censorship?" Kate asks.

"No!" says Allie, aghast at such a thought.

"Well, then you have to learn to live with a little smut."

A little smut? Women-in-bondage photofeatures, articles and letters encouraging incest and abuse, frequent cartoon and essay features that blaspheme God—these are standard fare today for even the "softest" and the most "respectable" of the pornographic magazines such as *Playboy* and *Penthouse*.

CBS says learn to live with it.

What Is Hollywood's Attitude?

One must wonder about the connection between what we see on TV and movie screens and what goes on in the city where most TV programs and movies are produced. Hollywood, known for its glitter, glamour, and stars, is leader in the child prostitution epidemic that plagues our nation. A news feature said the child prostitutes, some preteens, are everywhere along Hollywood Boulevard, sprinkled amid the business people and the tourists.

They are young, because that's what pays these days. At age 18, a prostitute is no longer desirable, according to psychologist Lois Lee who has established a program to help children get out of prostitution. While police efforts from time to time drive the trade indoors, or drive it from one area to another, it is a crime they have been unable to eliminate in Hollywood and surrounding areas.

To understand the depth and gravity of the problem, one need only observe the part of Hollywood prostitution which police haven't really addressed—the massive presence of teenage and preteen male prostitutes, mostly teens. They stand one or two to a corner, block after block, waiting for a car to slow down and someone to make an offer.

What is Hollywood's attitude toward pornography? One issue of *The Hollywood Reporter*, the voice of the film industry, was a special adult film issue. The magazine contained a special section promoting the pornography film industry, both movies and cable television. Nowhere in the entire publication was there a hint that there was a question of morality involved. In fact, the *Reporter* covered the issue in the same manner they would have covered a special Disney issue.

In Hollywood, the issue is already decided. A film is a film, and there is no difference between a pornographic film and a Disney film. They both make money, and that is the bottom line. Morality is no issue.

An ad bordering on child pornography (for Jet Set children's clothing) appeared in *The New York Times Magazine*. The ad portrayed a little girl six or seven years old, seductively posed, draped with a chain.

The banner across the top of the ad read, "We believe children should be seen as well as heard."

Adweek magazine critiqued the offensive ad this way: "Deering and Deering Advertising . . . capitalized on an unfortunate photographic composition here: the shadowy background, the languid gaze, the seductive pose with foot arched, leg lifted to bring attention to its shape. Giving the model a dog leash to hold across her thighs was a real mistake."

" 'Any offense was unintentional,' insisted Cheryl Deering of the ad agency ' . . . [and] we're not taking the blame,' " according to *Adweek*. Amazing! An ad agency poses a young girl in a sexually suggestive pose and drapes a chain across her body to try to sell children's clothing. They seem to acknowledge that it was in poor taste, but they insist they're not taking the blame. Surely it wasn't the child's idea!

The agency representative said they had received letters of complaint about the ad, but went on to ask, "What kind of people are writing these letters anyway?"

Another connection between pornography and the networks can be found in the experience of Sheila Nevins. She produced the sex-oriented cable TV program *Eros America*. Rejected by HBO, the program was aired on Cinemax. Miss Nevins described for *TV Guide* the gamut of sexual topics for *Eros America*, ranging from male strippers, prostitution, nude beaches, and sex before the big game (this portion suffered because baseball players wouldn't touch it). In *TV Guide*, Nevins defended the raunch of *Eros* by stating, "It would be as if we did a restaurant review and only reviewed good, wholesome restaurants as opposed to the greasy spoons." Nivens goes on to describe one program about a stripper/mother. "You say Cindy is a stripper; she's not a stripper. She's trying to make a living . . . she's trying to get a great house and get out of this dumb trailer park and she shows her body, y'know; is that different from some woman punching numbers in a supermarket who doesn't have such great breasts?"

Sheila Nevins is also a writer and producer at the Children's Television Workshop. These are the people who bring our children *Sesame Street*. The same *TV Guide* article said that Nevins was relieved when the production of the first cycle of shows for *Eros America* was complete because she could return to "working on a kid show."

Boycott "Ill Conceived"
Even some Christian publications exude ignorance concerning pornography. An editorial appeared in 1984 in the *United Meth-*

odist Reporter, the largest publication for United Methodists in America, stating that the boycott of 7-Eleven stores prior to their abandoning the sale of pornographic magazines in April 1986 was "ill conceived" and a diversion from the urgent task of combating "hard-core" materials that clearly meet the U.S. Supreme Court's definition of obscenity. The article went on to say that even a successful campaign against 7-Eleven's sale of such magazines as *Playboy* and *Penthouse* could hardly be considered a significant victory. The unmistakable implication of the comments is that *Playboy* and *Penthouse* are not the harmful varieties and that attention should be focused on the really dangerous "hard-core" magazines.

But the logic is faulty. According to March Bell in *The Pornography Revolution*, "evidence shows that the popular and least offensive pornography has been the most effective in achieving the goals of the sexual revolution. At the other end of the spectrum, the raunchy pornography of sadomasochism, bestiality, and so on has a lesser cultural impact and is more widely criticized."

Mr. Bell concludes that it is the popular pornography, the "soft-core" variety that has been most successful in undermining the Judeo-Christian consensus in our culture. The Playboy philosophy reduced to its simplest form is, according to Bell, "why should men endure the slow painful death of working to support an entire family when their goals can be achieved for the price of dinner and drinks?

"Playboy thus appeals to man's great temptation as regards marriage: to have its benefits without its responsibilities. The effects of such thinking have after 30-plus years of *Playboy* taken their toll on the psychology of individual males, especially since readership is now around 20 million. Modern pornographic man has rejected God and His law in favor of unbridled spontaneous humanism." Without doubt, *Playboy* is in the business of socially restructuring society.

Bell goes on to describe *Playboy* as "perhaps *the most diabolically well-crafted lifetime manual* for every possible male activity.

"Popular pornographic magazines, especially *Playboy* and *Penthouse* for men and *Cosmopolitan* for women, constantly offer exciting testimonies of varied new sexual experiences usually to be adopted or at least considered by the readership. *Penthouse* accomplishes this through its *Forum* section (also a separate publication). Each month numerous sexual conquests are erotically recounted to assure the reader that men and women everywhere are trying new partners, places, techniques, and so on to enhance sexual experiences. In related articles, a scientific support team of medical advisors with university credentials reassures the reader that healthy sexual experience can be enhanced by wife swapping, bisexuality, . . . and the like.

"'*Playboy* offers the reader a different way to think about how to spend money. It simply is cheaper to obtain sex than to enhance the growth and development of a family," says Bell.

Hard-core sex magazines are harmful. That no one doubts. But those who assume that the battle against *Playboy* and *Penthouse* is ill-conceived or misguided, as the *United Methodist Reporter* editorial stated, are sadly misinformed. The social cost of the *Playboy* world has been tremendous, especially in the area of divorce. And is it any wonder? What is the goal of the *Playboy* lifestyle? It certainly is *not* a multidimensional loving relationship. The goal is achievement of orgasm. Bell said: "A marriage relationship is expensive both economically and personally. The playboy is told that only orgasm is important and orgasm is far less costly than marriage." To target the *Playboy* plague is no diversion. It's front-line combat.

A Royko Tale

Not all the media treat pornography in a flippant manner. Popular columnist Mike Royko wrote not long ago about an incident from a past generation when a pornographer tried to function in a respectable Chicago neighborhood. It seems that he was a legitimate photographer, but began selling nude photos on the side. The people in the neighborhood didn't know about his sexy picture business until he made the mistake of asking a local teenage girl to model.

She told her mother. Her mother told her father. The father and his son went to the pornographer's home and knocked on the door with baseball bats.

A few weeks later the pornographer showed up at the local grammar school graduation to take photos of the young graduates. The teenager's father, still infuriated, proceeded to disrupt the graduation ceremony by explaining to his neighbors that the photographer was, in reality, a degenerate, sleazy, secretive pervert who should not even be allowed to live in their community.

Who was the hero? The angry father, that's who. (Remember, now, this was a generation or so ago.) Within two days of the graduation incident, the photographer had moved from the neighborhood and was never seen there again.

Who would be the hero today? The angry father in Royko's tale provides stark contrast to those who champion the same moral causes today. Let a man today reveal a pornographer for what he really is, and many in the media world ridicule and belittle the man, and try to laugh him out of respectability.

Let a man attack the hedonistic, self-centered values of *Playboy*'s Hugh Hefner or *Penthouse*'s Bob Guccione, and the man is labeled a right-wing, bigoted, unbalanced moral fascist. Hefner and Guccione are placed on pedestals and admired by the media liberals for bringing their anti-Christian philosophies into prominence. Isn't it interesting the direction which the liberal media elite have taken in the last 20 years. And they want the rest of us to follow their lead.

An editorial in the *Miami Voice* took a different point of view from that commonly expressed by the national secular media:

> All of a sudden America is shocked and frightened over headlines about sexual child abuse. Parents are bewildered and afraid to leave their children at local day care centers. Hasty townhouse meetings are being called. New laws are discussed, safeguards demanded.
>
> Sexual perversion of the lowest form has come to town!

Right in our own neighborhoods! Many people are baffled and angry.

Yet, we would have to ask some of our fellow citizens, why are you so surprised? And who should you be angry at?

Many of the people who are now crying out righteously about sexual abuse are the same ones who demand liberty and freedom of speech for an industry that sells sexual perversion as entertainment.

How many of these citizens have dirty movies depicting simulated or real sexual acts coming into their homes via cable or ON-TV? How many of us support the *Hustlers* and *Penthouses* and *Playboys* of the world which amass fortunes portraying people, especially women, as sexual toys? And don't forget Hollywood, the industry which ranks its products into various levels of sex and violence with a rating, not to keep kids out so much as to justify making them in the first place (just go to any R-rated movie and watch the 15- and 16-year-olds going in).

As for the X rating on movies and lock boxes for TV sets with dirty-movie access, which are supposed to keep young eyes from seeing what goes on behind closed doors—this is about as obscene as the movies themselves, because it is telling the young people that their parents and other mature "adults" believe it is OK to use for entertainment something which is too sleazy for children to behold.

How, then, can those same adults tell their growing children to respect their bodies and each other and to use restraint in sexual matters and to uphold marriage and commitment and responsibility as a way of life? How can youth accept such values when adult society uses the opposite values as a basic form of entertainment?

How, then, with all this sexual exploitation assaulting us in the media, can we be surprised that there are people out there who will be willing to exploit easy victims such as children, by acting out their sexual urges of them?

We have been saying for years that pornography and

prostitution do have victims. But the courts have been so busy listening to the smut peddler lawyers' cry of censorship that judges were unwilling to invoke a common-sense ruling that the rights of all citizens to a decent entertainment environment in which to live and raise children is more paramount.

Yes, there will always be some perverts out there anyway, but as Cardinal Bernardin of Chicago told a pornography conference recently, "Pornography is not so much an *outlet* for the baser instincts of the person, but a *stimulant!*"

Perhaps now is the time for concerned parents and organizations to start demanding some restrictions on the entertainment industry, while the victims are manifest. And we are not talking about total sanitization of all sex or all violent action, but some restraint and some value orientation that will at least not give aid and comfort to child molesters.

And perhaps the next time a local mayor suggests that dirty films not be allowed on local television cable, he will not be hooted at quite so loudly by local secular media which now are so righteously concerned about sexual abuse.

An editorial in the Richmond, Virginia *News-Leader* put pornography in the proper perspective. The writer said that while public outcry over pornography usually centers on *Hustler* or other such crude and profane publications, *Playboy* may inflict the greater harm.

The editorial went on to say:

Playboy describes its centerfolds in adolescent prose. The girls list their favorite books and movies. They are shown walking to class, riding horses, and cooking dinner with Mom. They supposedly embody the fabled "girl next door."

They also take their clothes off for cameras. Don't such

pictures encourage voyeurs to believe that *all* girls are like centerfolds, that lurking within every pert cheerleader is an insatiable playmate with just one thing on her mind?

Generally the courts have stymied public efforts to promote public decency. . . . As a consequence of [pornography's] permeation seemingly everywhere, history may record that when the U.S. decided "anything goes," much of value got up and went.

Values determine what a person will and will not do. Few people seem to realize that the values held by many in the national secular liberal media are quite the opposite of those held by Christians.

William F. Fore, at the time Assistant General Secretary of Communication with the National Council of Churches and now General Secretary of Communication with the same group, wrote an article in 1977 for *Christian Century* titled "Mass Media's Mythic World: At Odds with Christian Values." He stated: "The whole weight of Christian history, thought, and teaching stands diametrically opposed to the media world and its values."

Perhaps that helps us to better understand the general attitude of the media toward pornography.

8.
A Political Scientist's View of Pornography

By Dr. Reo M. Christenson,
Professor of Political Science, Miami University, Oxford, Ohio

The pornographers of America should take warning! The winds of change are blowing. Pornographers, your days of wine and roses are fading. The public has seen what you do with the freedom you have been granted, and they don't like what they see. Nor do America's feminists. Nor do other women who care about their families, their community, and their country. Nor do many of America's leading intellectuals.

Let me start from square one. The Founding Fathers never intended for the First Amendment to be interpreted as the courts interpret it today. They were sensible men, resolved to protect the right of heretics and dissenters to expound their views on social, economic, political, and religious matters without fear of government reprisals. But they would have laughed to scorn any notion that *Hustler* magazine, vulgar T-shirts, naked dancers, and X-rated movies could hide behind the First Amendment. Nothing could have been further from their intentions.

The Supreme Court has never upheld the absolutist view that no restrictions can ever be imposed on speech or press. A score of marginal restraints exist, most of which are noncontroversial.

Nor has the Court ever conceded that obscene material is protected by the First Amendment. But the Court has made two glaring errors. First, it took a long leap and gave commercial entertainment as much constitutional protection as political discourse. Well, almost. Then it tried to reconcile its exclusion of obscenity with its protection of commercial entertainment by setting up interpretive roadblocks which make effective enforcement of antiobscenity laws next to impossible.

The pornographers have exploited this opening by employing expensive—very expensive—and unscrupulous lawyers concerned with nothing but the bottom line. Prosecutors are usually no match for these legal hit men, skilled as they are at throwing sand in jurors' eyes. The pornographers have also used the American Civil Liberties Union as its front line of defense. The strategy has been brilliant, successful—and disastrous to those who care about the quality of life in their communities.

In Minneapolis and Indianapolis, feminists have sought to deal with *some* aspects of pornography by declaring it violates women's civil rights and jeopardizes their prospects for obtaining genuine equality. They are doomed to fail. They have come too close to saying that speech which is deemed to be socially harmful has no constitutional protection. The implications are too broad, and I regret that I cannot support the language employed by the well-intentioned people who drafted the language of these statutes. Chances are slim that the courts will accept such law.

They should have used a more direct, straightforward approach. They should have sought a new federal law which banned the movement in interstate commerce of any material real or simulated, or any performance which involves visually explicit sexual behavior, intended for commercial entertainment.

This could be defined as any performance or material which visually depicts ultimate sexual acts, including intercourse, sodomy, cunnilingus, fellatio, analingus, and masturbation, where the penetration or ejaculation of the genital organs is visible. And that, I might add, would largely dispose of the nagging problem of statutory vagueness. And with the uncertainties involved in *Miller vs. California:* "patently offensive," "appeals to the prurient interest," "the work taken as a whole" and the "LAPS" test.

They should have argued that such entertainment is outside the orbit of constitutional protection because it does not contribute to the kind of social discourse which the Founding Fathers had in mind *or* which a reasonable interpretation of its purpose, in a democratic society, would justify.

Pornography, remember, is an appeal to the viscera which bypasses the mind rather than being a serious attempt to contribute to reasoned or illuminating discussion of matters of social importance. Whatever its "message," that message is no more than subliminal. That does not mean it may not be powerful, but it does mean it is not the sort of thing the First Amendment is obligated to protect. People don't feed on pornography to be intellectually nourished, and they aren't! They want raw meat and that's what they get.

They should, then, have noted that the Supreme Court has always permitted *reasonable* restrictions on *marginal* aspects of speech and press, e.g., laws forbid perjury, libel, incitement to violence, divulging military secrets, advocating federal strikes, making obscene, threatening, or harassing phone calls, advertising cigarettes on TV, fraudulent ads, and many more. Indeed, the First Amendment itself limits free speech by implicitly forbidding religious indoctrination in public schools.

The point is that pornography falls squarely into this category of expected speech and press that is not allowable.

Nor are the essential elements of speech and press impaired so long as those who would challenge existing laws and moral codes are free to publish and circulate, by whatever appeals to reason they can muster, their case for abolishing the family, or eliminating legal restraints on any kind of sexual behavior. They have a right to make this case, no matter how painful it may be to the rest of us. But [they should make their case] through an attempted appeal to reason, not through visual entertainment which assaults the very core of mankind's concern for decency and which scorns a fair fight in the marketplace of ideas. That's a fight they cannot win. There isn't a legislature in our 50 states willing to repeal all laws against obscene materials.

That pornography is a marginal aspect of speech and press cannot, it seems to me, be denied. But are the proposed restraints reasonable? Yes, because of the damage we can reasonably expect pornography to do.

Let me back up a bit. The President's Commission on Pornography and Obscenity in 1970 issued a voluminous report which concluded that there was no persuasive empirical evidence that such material led to antisocial behavior.

That report has been cited ten thousand times in the press. What the public does not know is that no social scientist, to my knowledge, has reexamined the report and found it defensible. It has been denounced by outstanding social scientists, psychologists, and journalists—none of whom believe it met the test of scientific objectivity. I do not have time to enumerate its flaws, but if you wish, you can consult the analyses of Lane Sunderland, Leonard Berkowitz, Harry Clor, Victor Cline, James Q. Wilson, and Garry Wills.

Well, things are much worse today than they were in 1970. We have had a scandalous outpouring of child pornography, which is currently on the defensive but has by no means been eliminated. We have an avalanche of material featuring sadomasochistic sexual behavior, an avalanche which was predicted all along by realists who were skeptical of all the talk about people getting bored if only they had free access to pornography. And not only by sadomasochistic stuff but also by every form of bizarre, grotesque, and shameless imagery which depraved minds can concoct.

I agree with Professor James Wilson of Harvard who states that social science does not have sufficiently sensitive and sophisticated techniques and tools for definitively proving what damage pornography does or does not do. Especially when it comes to its long-range impact and its impact on people who are not emotionally healthy and hence are particularly prone to commit antisocial acts. I might add that science can't tell us whether love is better than hatred, democracy better than dictatorship, peace better than war, or about anything else in the realm of values—that is, in the things that matter most.

But if science cannot give us assured answers, let us use our common sense. Pornography leaves the impression with its viewers that sex has no relationship to privacy, that it is unrelated to love, commitment or marriage, that bizarre forms of sex are the most gratifying, that sex with animals has a specially desirable flavor, and that irresponsible sex has no adverse consequences—no venereal disease, illegitimate births, abortions, premature marriages, single-parent families, or moral erosion. I see no way that a torrent of materials with this subliminal message, which ultimately fans out to reach people of almost all ages, can fail to have pernicious effects. As has often been said, if destructive material can do no harm, then constructive material can do no good—and everything conscientious parents have believed since the dawn of the family is wrong.

Not that someone sees pornography and then rushes out to commit rape. That may happen, though that's not the main problem. But whatever conditions people to regard destructive sexual behavior as harmless, or worse, as desirable, will inevitably weaken those barriers which society erects against irresponsible sexual conduct. If this is not true, then black is white and up is down.

It is interesting that while a dozen studies have demonstrated that violent entertainment stimulates violent behavior on the part of those who witness it, entertainment featuring irresponsible sexual behavior is alleged to have no effect on its consumers.

I would emphasize the significance of the study by professors at the University of Indiana and the University of Evansville showing that persons who see a lot of pornography believe rapists should be treated more indulgently than those who don't. Charles Peters summarized earlier research from Purdue, Colorado, Wisconsin, and Manitoba as indicating that violent pornography inspires violence. Peters added, "This strikes me as about as surprising as the news that hungry men want to eat." And *Newsweek* reported on the University of Wisconsin study which showed that sexually violent films like *The Texas Chainsaw*

Massacre make men more likely to accept the notion that women enjoy rape. It also reported a UCLA study demonstrating that men exposed to violent pornography show an increased willingness to inflict pain on women.

Conclusive proof? No. Persuasive evidence? Yes.

If, then, we can reasonably assume that a flood of pornography will gradually erode barriers against irresponsible sex, what are the ultimate implications? Here I would like to cite a highly significant study made 50 years ago by Professor J.D. Unwin of Cambridge, a study in which the author found the opposite of what he hoped to find. (That always impresses me, because it is so easy for social scientists to formulate a study, or interpret its findings, to get the results they want.)

After examining the sexual practices of more than 80 primitive and more advanced societies, Unwin concluded that sexually permissive behavior led to less cultural energy, less creativity, less individualism, less mental development, and less cultural progress in general. Primitive societies with the greatest sexual freedom had made the least cultural advances. Those with stricter limitations had made the greatest progress. Among civilized societies, the same rule held. Those with restrictive sexual codes had made the greatest cultural strides, and when more permissive sexual standards appeared, cultural decline set in. Unwin said there was no known instance of a society that restrained as high a cultural level after relatively relaxed sexual standards replaced more rigorous ones (although he conceded that it might take several generations before the debilitating effect was clearly manifest).

William Stephens, after studying 90 primitive cultures, wrote that the tribes lowest on the scale of cultural evolution have the most sexual freedom. Sigmund Freud, surprisingly to some, associated cultural advances with limitations on sexual activity. Arnold Toynbee, celebrated student of world civilizations, declared that a culture which postpones rather than stimulates sexual experience in the young is a culture most prone to progress. Will and Ariel Durant, after a lifetime of studying world history, wrote in *The Lessons of History* that it was imperative to maintain rigorous sexual restraints upon the young.

Again, this does not constitute irrefutable proof. But it is surely evidence worthy of respect—and it would have received that respect, and widespread publicity, if only its findings had been what liberals wanted to hear. That is why most of you have never heard of it.

So we aren't talking about trivial matters here; we are getting down to bedrock. Since the widespread circulation of pornography is doubtless an important factor in subverting cultural barriers against irresponsible sex, there are solid grounds for our concern.

Do we have a religious obligation to fight pornography? I think we do. Can you imagine what the outspoken prophets of the Old Testament would have said if they could witness the kind of debauchery that floods our newsstands and postal channels and X-rated theaters and video cassettes? Is there any doubt what their attitude would be? No wonder the American Jewish Congress has expressed concern about the growth of pornography.

What would the Apostle Paul have said about the current scene, the same Paul who denounced the sexual licentiousness of his day? Would he have said, "Condemn it, but then shrug your shoulders and walk away"? I don't think so. Should not Christians actively oppose grave social evils, especially when they are recognized as evils not only by Christians but by responsbile people of every religion and no religion?

To privately deplore but publicly ignore is to default on the responsibility we all have to promote the well-being of our community and our country. Certainly Christians are not exempt from this obligation.

Happily, we have allies today which not long ago were not with us. Feminists, although often intimidated by the ACLU, are up in arms about pornography. They see beyond the superficial and glib arguments of porn's defenders to the heart of what is really involved.

I might add that the ACLU has done many constructive things during its history. It has fought some noble battles for the Bill of Rights. Occasionally, it still does. But it has become shrill, dogmatic, and closed-minded on the issue of pornography. It cavalierly ignores the arguments of those who disagree with it, and it insists that the freedoms we all cherish will be gravely imperiled if *Hustler* is hustled off the scene. No censorship, it cries, hoping that buzz word will frighten people from exercising independent thought in this field.

Well, let me tell you something. Almost everyone in America believes in censorship, including those who think they don't.

What sensible person believes that a community would exceed its proper authority if it denied a license to an entertainment troupe which wanted to exhibit men lashing women with whips for their sexual pleasure, operating on the principle that women as well as men can relish sexually related pain if only they have the proper perspective? What sensible person thinks a community would exceed its proper boundaries if it forbade a license for entertainers to perform live sex on stage? And all of those who vow "no censorship" want to censor child pornography.

The truth is, then, that almost everyone believes in censorship, including newspaper editors who say they don't, and a lot of ACLU members who think they don't. They just draw the line at a different point.

So much, then, for those who say, "See what you want to see and turn away from what you disapprove, but don't tell others what they can and cannot see." People who say that haven't thought things through.

Parenthetically, doctrinaire liberals are often monotheists. They worship only one god and its name is the ACLU. When this deity speaks, they reverently genuflect, suspend their critical judgment, and parrot its lines. They feel very smug and superior to the great unenlightened masses who, being clear-eyed rather than dogma-ridden, regard pornography as a disgrace which ought to be curbed.

Note I said *doctrinaire* liberals, not all liberals. On many issues, I am more liberal than conservative, so I don't want to be misunderstood.

It is often implied that only yahoos and Puritans worry about pornography or favor its censorship. Well, listen to this.

Irving Kristol, co-editor of the *Public Interest* and columnist for the *Wall Street Journal,* favors it. Charles Peters, editor of the respected *Washington Monthly,* says, "Pornography seems clearly outside the realm of political discourse—while the argument that we should have the right to publish pornography is clearly within it." (That's precisely what I'm saying.) Peters further states that the censorship of violent pornography on TV "does not bother me in the least, and I am astonished by the legal minds who cannot distinguish between it and the censorship of political discussion. . . . "

James Fallows, political editor of one of the nation's most prestigious magazines, *The Atlantic,* asks, "Can't we use common sense, if not First Amendment absolutism, to agree on the difference between political beliefs and sexual services? Can't we find a way to ensure the Klan's right to march and the Communists' right to organize without waiving our culture's right to shape its moral environment?"

In a recent issue of *Harper's* magazine, editor Lewis Lapham observes that Americans "have insisted on the right to free speech . . . to the point of confusing it with pornography. . . . " Charles Krauthammer, an editor of the *New Republic,* wrote a recent essay in *Time* in which he said, "Many are prepared to make expression a bit less free in order to make their community a bit more whole, or as skeptics might say, wholesome. That is nothing to be ashamed of."

Henry Fairlie, another contributing editor to the *New Republic,* says that liberals "have abetted the perversion of the First Amendment until it is used to protect the peddlers of filth."

Norman Podhoretz, editor of *Commentary,* wrote that "Committed indiscriminately . . . to free speech, on what grounds of principle could [liberals] stand against the tidal wave of hardcore pornography. . . ?"

Identifying himself with those who place a high value on community life, Professor Michael J. Sandel of Harvard says, "Communitarians would be more likely than liberals to allow a town to ban porno bookstores, on the grounds that pornography offends the way of life and the values that sustain it."

George Kennan, initiator of America's long-maintained "containment" policy, lists pornography as one of the most serious threats America faces from within.

Finally, George Will, in *Statecraft as Soulcraft*, writes that, "Even more injurious than the flood of obscenity that has been let loose have been the arguments for letting it loose."

Some yahoos! Some Puritans!

Not all of these would extend censorship as far as some of us would, but these citations should illustrate the point that many intellectuals are either allies or potential allies of our cause.

I think the time has come to act. It is time to confront presidential and congressional candidates with a proposal to ban from interstate commerce material or performances which involve visually explicit sexual behavior intended for commercial entertainment, and it is time to force them to take a stand. Time for the nation to realize, for the courts to realize, that communities have a right to set minimal standards of decency.

The licentiousness of modern pornographers has become a stench in our nostrils. The age of unbridled individualism, of individualism *uber alles*, is fading, the attitude that "I want to do what I want to do and see what I want to see and if the community doesn't like it, it can go suck its thumb"—that is passing. An age which seeks a more sensible balance between the rights of the individual and the rights of the community is already on its way. Let us work to hasten its coming.

9.
A Message to the Church

All of us, I trust, are united in the battle against the corruption of the social environment by porno-violence, in the battle to keep America civilized. This battle has two fronts, each related to the other.

The first battlefront, with all of its problems and dangers, has to do with the law and our demand that the law protect our communities and children from moral filth. What else can do it? It is not easy to say this, for who likes censorship? But surely if the law and the educational power of the State are rightly used to protect our physical health and environment (pure food laws, regulations against polluting of air and water, etc.), surely the law cannot be unconcerned at the pollution of the moral atmosphere. We must love freedom and civility, and we must not be impressed when some suggest that the Founding Fathers fought to make the world safe for the pornographers. It is not easy to combine freedom and law, but it must be done unless we are to become the corrupted corrupters of the world.

Is the government so gentle, the laws so permissive, tolerance so complete, that we permit (as in Times Square) the under world, vice, and pornography to take over the social scene? Does the Constitution of the United States mean that the pornographers may strut in the marketplace and corrupt the nations? Do we protect against war and water pollution and not against moral pollution? Is there physical infection but no moral corruption? With all of its difficulties, the law is the main battleground.

The second front is that of public opinion, the battle for the public mind. It is an intellectual battle, a recognition that the corruption of a people begins in its thinking, a duty on our part to make it clear that pornography is really evil stuff and a great danger, our duty to arouse the public conscience so that in anger the people say "Enough is enough." To show that pornography is a new and dangerous evil is the purpose of this essay.

Nothing like this has ever before been faced by any civilization, because the technical means of broadcasting porno-violence (TV, films, the art of photography and printing) were lacking. Moreover, what we are witnessing is a new thing, because the growth or rise of massive cities with their rootless populations is also new. Most of the world until the modern era has been rural, agricultural, conservative, held in line by old and honored customs and by social restraints. Today, we have not only the media, but the mass media appealing to the masses in the often rootless anonymity of our cities. I repeat that this is a new danger in a new civilization. So if someone says we have always had pornography and points to some book that a European aristocrat kept under lock and key, don't be fooled by that stuff. We are not talking about a single book under lock and key, loaned by one man to friends; we are talking about big business, mass distribution—about pornography that struts in the marketplace, about the so-called "right" of sleazy characters to corrupt the moral atmosphere of an entire nation.

Second, pornography involving children, sex with animals and every perversion is now backed by big money, the organized underworld, and there are quick fortunes being made. When our society became permissive and the law looked the other way, big and evil forces moved into the social vacuum. There is mass production and highly organized distribution behind this. A *New*

York Times study revealed that 70 to 90 percent of pornography comes from the underworld, and since only a person in the underworld, who would do anything for money, would film such things, those statistics are easy to believe.

When, therefore, a self-serving appeal to "rights" and "freedom" is made by the pornographers, we must remember that the "freedom" they desire is the "right" to distribute filth from coast to coast, to corrupt and to subvert, until—as revealed in New York City and Boston—centers of pornography become centers of vice.

What about sex? Are we justified in being outraged, shocked, angry over what is happening? Or are we simply prudish and repressed? Here, from our heritage and from the experience of the race are some observations on sex.

It comes from the Creator's hand and, therefore, it is good. "And God saw everything that He had made and behold it was good."

It is powerful in all nature because the future of a species depends on it.

Sex stands somewhat at the mysterious center of our personalities, protected by a sense of modesty and shame. Because of the intimacy connected with sex, this modesty and shame are universal in every advanced culture and can be seen in the architecture of our houses where, in contrast to the living rooms, we place doors on bedrooms and bathrooms. Indeed a barbarian is a person without civilized restraints, who does in public what is meant to be done in private.

Our tradition at its best recognizes that sex is good, and powerful, and therefore it has kept sex somewhat in the background of life. Its power was recognized, but it was kept under control as one controls the blessings of fire. Doors, privacy, modesty, chaperones, standards—all of these were restraints upon a drive which, when unrestrained, led to tragedy.

Some say that humans should be "natural," forgetting that a person cannot be natural as is an animal, for the simple reason that an animal is completely governed by instinct. Civilized living is a thing of standards, restraints, courtesies, reason—a second nature imposed upon our raw nature. It is in a sense highly artificial when we mow our lawns, dust our homes, bathe our bodies, restrain our tempers, and discipline ourselves to work when we prefer to sleep. All of this, I repeat, is highly artificial, but it happens to be what we mean by civilization. We are most truly human, then, when we are self-controlled, disciplined, courteous, clean, respectful, and reasonable, not when we are governed by the whim of the moment.

In sex we see the necessity for standards and restraint, for in sex is clearly revealed the glory and tragedy of our human freedom. Man is in nature like any animal, but we are also "above" it and can in our freedom use this sexual nature correctly or corrupt it. We can use it wisely, beautifully, sacramentally, or we can use it as a tool of pride as we notch up conquests. We can utterly debase it in pornography, prostitution, perversion. No animal can rise so high or sink so low. The only thing that a person cannot do is to be natural like an animal, because a human being is not just an animal. And all this illustrates why from the wisdom of the race, we have inherited standards, caution, restraints, modesty, a wise placing of sex somewhat in the background of daily life.

If what we have inherited from our tradition contains wisdom, then in the modern world we are being very foolish, and we will pay for it. Yes, we are paying for it. The judgments of God upon us are not like bolts of lightning that have no relation to our conduct. No, this is a moral universe, and the judgments on us are the logical outcome of our actions. Look at some of the judgments that are becoming evident.

The deepest meaning of sex is not simply physical; it is also spiritual. Man is not only just body; he is body-spirit. Sex is sacramental; it expresses love, creates love, and unites spirits. In marriage two become one.

When, therefore, in pornography the sex act is photographed, it cannot avoid being bestial for the simple reason that love, the spirit, the inner meaning of sex cannot possibly be photographed. Pornography, then, is a caricature of human sex, a corruption, an obvious bestializing of a central and important aspect of life; and that corruption and bestializing will not remain confined to sex.

We have said that our tradition teaches restraint, self-control, the channeling of sex in marriage. It teaches continence. It teaches that sex is not the casual satisfaction of appetite, as one eats or drinks. If we remove the restraints and sex becomes a casual thing, like a drink of water, then there will be ugly results, such as venereal disease in epidemic proportions. It would be helpful if we could get it through our heads as people that everything has its price. "The fear of the Lord is the beginning of wisdom" (Prov. 1:7). Venereal disease is, of course, a medical problem, but it is also a moral problem. If promiscuity is encouraged, taught, promoted from coast to coast, with vice inevitably gathering around pornography, how does a nation avoid the spread of venereal disease?

Our tradition is right in seeing that man needs no sexual stimulation, rather the contrary. Since human desire is not confined to a mating season but is a year-long matter, sex should be in the background of life. Pornography does two things: (1) It stimulates—that is its chief purpose as revealed by the fact that vice and prostitution gather around it; and (2) it stresses the physical so much that it becomes difficult for some people to remember and recognize that behind all that flesh is a person, a soul, a human being to be honored and respected.

Therefore, we are witnessing in our society an increase in rapes, which will continue until we return to the deeper wisdom of our tradition.

It is truly amazing that the women of America in their present campaigns have not made the pornographers their number one enemy. It is also amazing that many leaders in our society do not see the connection between pornography and rape.

Some will argue that the connection between pornography and rape cannot be proved scientifically; of course, it cannot, nor can it be scientifically disproved. This simply reveals that the scientific method is inadequate in this matter.

How in the complexity of life today, with perhaps a broken home, no religious training, questionable friends, a permissive atmosphere, an unstable personality, can you prove a particular piece of pornography led to a particular rape? Of course you cannot prove it or disprove it. So the thing to do is to sit back in our chairs and think with the brains God gave us.

What do you think is going to happen if, by powerful media from coast to coast, you stimulate a desire that needs no stimulation, bring into the forefront of life what should by reason be somewhat in the background, and corrupt the imagination of the people? What do you think is going to happen?

It is said that obscenity is in the eye of the beholder. E.J. Mishan asks, "Is cruelty also, then, in the eye of the beholder?" Is dishonesty only in the eye of the beholder? Are moral standards simply a matter of taste, so that it is impossible to identify what is corrupt, debasing, pornographic, and obscene? Is everything subjective? Nonsense!

All of us share a common human nature and a firsthand and immediate knowledge of the creation and its purposes. We have an objective standard in the nature we did not create and out of which we cannot stir. Are there reasonable standards for driving a car, for handling money, for the health of the body? Are there wise rules for the use of our eyes, hearts, and lungs but not for sex? If a person shrugs his shoulders about pornography, is that tolerant or degenerate? Is our society with its "spectator sex" progressive or corrupt? If sex has its lovely place in life, as it most surely does, does that not also mean that it can get out of place? Can we be so deluged with the subject that, as when there is too much smoke, we speak of air pollution, so, when there is too much sex, we can speak of a sex-polluted society? I repeat: sex has its good and God-given place in life, but it can get out of place; and keeping things in their proper places is one way of expressing what we mean by civilization.

Finally, in our tradition, we cherish the family—as the Prayer Book puts it, "The homes in which Thy people dwell." Yes! and by nature, the family is in all the world the fundamental unit of society, the basis of a stable society, a school of virtue, a training ground of character. A Pope said these words: "The family was ordained by God that children might be trained up for

Himself—it was before the church, or rather the first form of the church on earth."

The family is in trouble for many sociological reasons (our mobility, rootless, etc.) but one of the most vicious attacks on the family comes from corrupting pornography. We all remember reading about the outraged mothers in a section of Detroit who picketed the pornographic shops, because (God bless them) they wanted their homes protected from this evil that could destroy them. When the home goes, everything else begins to go.

Broken homes produce, or tend to produce, troubled people. But we sometimes forget that love of country is also weakened. Charles Dickens said, "In love of home, the love of country has its rise." In the last verse of our national anthem, we sing, "And thus be it ever when true men shall stand, between their loved homes and the war's desolation. . . ."

The home is the school of virtue and it is simple truth to see that we love America because we love the small subdivisions of home, family, and neighbors in which life has placed us. America, from Maine to Hawaii, from Florida to Alaska, is simply too big to comprehend and too vast to love. We love America because of "the hills of home" and because of the little intimate subdivisions that are in our hearts.

Pornography is subversive of America itself, and for that reason we can call upon the power of government and of the law to protect our country from this evil.

10.
The Victim's View of Pornography

By Rt. Rev. Richard S. Emrich,
Episcopal Bishop (retired)

Almost daily I receive letters from victims of pornography graphically telling how pornography takes its toll on people. Included in this chapter are some of these letters. They vividly illustrate the fact that pornography is addictive and harmful. Though rarely do we get unsigned letters from victims of pornography, these letters, however, are edited to insure anonymity, and names have been omitted.

DEAR MR. WILDMON:
At 17 years of age, I enlisted in the Army in a desperate attempt to find meaning and purpose for my life. I went on to graduate from jump school and served as a paratrooper with the 82nd Airborne Division. For a while it looked like I had a bright future ahead of me, but instead of finding myself, I got lost in a world of alcohol, drugs, and vice of every sort. I began frequenting topless discos, X-rated movie houses, and massage parlors. I had many sexual encounters with prostitutes during this time, and on several occasions I engaged in sexual acts which I'm ashamed to talk about.

This exposure to moral corruption had such an influence on my personality that I eventually lost respect for myself or for other people. My self-image was totally shattered. The high

Christian values that my parents had tried to instill in me were thrown to the wind. I reached a point where I just didn't care any more. My lifestyle confirmed that I was morally warped, a pervert; otherwise, I reasoned, I wouldn't have been living the way I was at the time. It got so that the more involved I became in vice the more perverted I felt, and the more perverted I felt, the more deeply I engaged in vice almost as if it were to confirm my self-image. Eventually, I reached the point where I threw in the towel.

In 1975 I went on a crime spree during which I had a major part in brutally murdering four innocent people. I'm now serving life in prison, and I blame pornography for much of my downfall. Its influence on my personality was awesome. While I am personally responsible for the crimes I committed, pornography helped bring me to the point where I didn't care any more and thus enabled me to slip to the point where I was actually a participant in four bloody murders.

I understand that you are going to be participating in a Justice Department study on the effects of pornography. If I can help in any way, including actually testifying before Congress, please feel free to call on me. Having lived in the gutter, I can tell you from firsthand experience that it stinks. I salute what you are trying to accomplish, and I am willing to do what I can to assist in this worthwhile effort.

God bless you!

DEAR MR. WILDMON:
First, I am a 53-year-old male, and in January 1982 I was arrested and charged with third-degree sodomy. I was tried and found guilty and sentenced to 30 days in jail and five years probation.

What I would like to contribute is the fact that pornography played a primary role in my seduction of young children. Over a 15- to 20-year period I used what I consider as dirty and filthy material to arouse young boys and girls. Things or material I used consisted of magazines, snapshots, and 8mm movies.

I found that magazines such as *Playboy, Penthouse,* and

Hustler worked very well for my devious seduction of young children. Also I found this same material would arouse and stimulate myself.

I personally feel material such as I have named and the more filthy material that I used to subscribe to contributed a great deal to the problem that people like myself have. This says nothing to the damage, through my actions, that has been done to countless young children.

I feel too that young children who come into contact with pornography on their own are greatly harmed. They can't help but get a distorted picture of sex and sexuality.

I thank God that I have a Christ to whom I owe my new life.

I am presently in secular therapy but consider the church as my best source of help. I was very fortunate and was accepted as I was by many good Christian people.

Also, if I can be of any service to you on this matter in any way, please let me know. There is so much to be said, but I don't want to take up too much of your time. I hope you can make out my writing and this letter will be of some service in the Lord's battle with this cancer that seems to be growing in our beautiful country.

Mr. Wildmon, my prayers are with you and thank you for your time.

DEAR MR. WILDMON:
I was a victim of pornography by the man I was married to. He read nothing but *Hustler* and *Playboy*. I was subjected to forced sex along with abnormal sexual acts for the year I was with him. I was also attacked by physical abuse that left me bruised mentally and physically. He also had sexual relationships with young men that he allowed to live with us.

At this time I was not a Christian, but I had never been exposed to such abnormalities. I was going to commit suicide, and it was then that I received Jesus Christ as my Saviour.

Twice I have been exposed to down-and-out sexual intercourse on TV during prime time while at another person's house, and their children were watching it. Unless this is removed from

TV and in magazines, the sexual victims percentage will continue.

It is time that we all join together to fight against this and win. I am willing to join with you in this fight.

BROTHER WILDMON:
As a child of the King, I regret to say that I have had a more direct dealing with pornography than I wish to admit. Most of it came before I accepted Christ two years ago, but even after that the demon of pornography would not let go.

It all began when I was just a young boy (I am now 38). I would go to the nearest convenience store and, out of curiosity more than anything, look at the stag magazines. But at that time they had the "decency" to blot out the more private female parts with an ink blot. After a while, though, they got bolder. Anyway, those curious looks led to more curious looks. The next thing I knew I was looking at the amusement page of the newspaper to see revealing pictures of the movies that were showing in the Houston metropolis. The Houston papers were more vivid in their movie advertisement section. I went from the newspapers to the Sears catalog. All the time I was being programmed. The more bare skin I could see on a female body, the better I liked it.

That desire went from the catalog to making trips to the public library to read vivid accounts of a private detective's encounter with some glamorous blonde or brunette. Depending on which private detective's novel I was reading, some of these detectives' encounters with these girls were more vivid than others. Brother Wildmon, I was reading these books and being desensitized in a public library all because of some curious looks at the pornography when I was a young boy.

Anyway, as I became older, the pornography got bolder. My "innocent" curiosity grew as I got involved with the bolder pornography. The pornography led to vivid imagination and some of the filthiest of fantasies. As I got older, I graduated from high school, bought me a car, and could come and go from my family's home as I pleased. All the time this was happening, I was being introduced to hard-core pornography. The hard-core was displaying sexually explicit scenes. That opened up an unhealthy sexual appetite that could not be satisfied. My imagination and my fantasies were filled with perversion.

Finally, as I became more independent, the desire for the hard-core pornographic magazines and novels graduated to the X-rated movies. I attended one of these movies at least once a week. It seemed like every time the feature changed at this particular movie house, I was there to see the newest X-rated movie. Then the desire for X-rated movies graduated to the real thing. I began to visit topless bars, where the female dancers were either topless or totally nude. They would engage in suggestive dances that would leave little to the imagination. And believe me, with my warped and perverted imagination, I could fill in what little was left out.

I wish I could share with you some of my most vivid imaginations and some of the most perverted fantasies, but I must go on.

My desire for the sexually explicit and my lust for bare skin on the female body has carried over into my married life. I am now separated from my family and part of that I blame on the demon of pornography and the evil spirits associated with its particular lust.

Brother Wildmon, let me share with you the brand marks left on me by pornography. I cannot take a casual glance at a young lady with any bare skin showing without taking a hard second look to see if there's more the second time. If I see the least bit of bare skin on a female, I have an automatic urge to see more.

I used to drive a full size pick-up for work purposes. My idea of a good day was to drive alongside a young lady's car and see what she was or was not wearing—the less the better, and the shorter the dress or shorts, the better. Human nature might think and say this is natural, but in my case because of the desire of the sexually explicit and the perverted lust for bare skin, given me by the demon of pornography, this "natural desire" is exaggerated.

Brother Don, I mentioned that I accepted Christ two years ago. May I too say that the demon of pornography did not let me go even then, except for a little while.

I accepted Christ in August 1983. In the early part of December of that same year, pornography again took its unnatural hold. I got a cash advance of $75 on a MasterCard. I then directly went to Houston, Texas and spent the whole $75 on a combination of sexually explicit "peep" shows and an all-nude girl dancing establishment.

However, to my knowledge, that was my last contact with the sexually explicit or hard-core pornography. That is not to say that I do not still have evil urges. True, an all-loving Christ has delivered me from that demon, but the brand marks of sin will, I suppose, always be there. Even now the few times I watch TV, my eyes are mostly drawn to the juicier scenes such as in the bedroom.

I suppose the brand marks of pornography and the sexually explicit will always be with me in my mind, but I do know this, it's by the grace of an all-loving God that I'm not spending time in a federal or state penitentiary for the crime of rape or sexual assault of some sort. Believe me because of pornography I've had the "education."

Brother Don, I'm sorry about the length of this letter. Perhaps I could have edited it a little better, but I felt the more detail the better. I did not go into detail on my more perverted fantasies and imaginations. I am just ashamed to tell you that I have had them.

If you can use this lengthy letter or wish to edit it to better make a point to expose the truth about the demon of pornography, please feel free to do so. I shamefully wrote this letter, but even though full of shame, I hope it can be used for the honor and glory of God. I don't want any praise. I choose to believe I wrote this letter under God's direction. I wish your organization power and strength from God's use of this letter. To Him be the glory. Thank you for allowing me to take a stand against this evil demon of pornography.

DEAR MR. WILDMON:
I was deeply involved in pornography from 15 to 25 years of

age. Starting with what I thought was innocent reading and pictures from magazines such as *Penthouse* and *Playboy*, my life, my mind was not my own.

I could not pass a covenience store without asking my boyfriend to stop in and get me the new issue. I took it to his house, read it from cover to cover, and then what? What would I do with my mind filled with all types of sexual action, some "so-called normal" and some quite bizarre?

Well, I performed oral sex with my boyfriend's dog. I tried to force my neighbor's three-year-old child to perform oral sex on me. He refused. I was 15.

My sex life with my boyfriend, then my husband, was not untouched by pornography. I could not climax without hearing filth said to me or have it in my mind. I also fantasized all the times we had sex about other guys—black ones, my own father, my brother, a sexual train, rape, children, etc. I was controlled by my thoughts.

I cheated on my husband two times in the first three years of our marriage. It was never good enough just with him; my mind wouldn't let it be.

I am free from pornography today. Jesus has control of my thoughts, not pornography.

Get pornography off the shelves of stores and throw it in the garbage where it belongs.

DEAR MR. WILDMON:

I am a victim of pornography. Over a three-year period I spent hundreds and hundreds of dollars on *Playboy*, *Penthouse*, and whatever else was on sale.

I was addicted to it. I bought it for one reason only—sexual excitement.

After a while, *Playboy* was not explicit enough. I wanted more and more. I even bought *Hustler*. I would have bought anything sold.

I knew that buying and looking and reading these magazines was wrong for me, but I was addicted.

I have not bought a magazine for about five years, but I am

still an addict. Every time I see the magazines in a store or on the Atlanta airport newsstand, I have to fight with all my might to keep from buying one. I wish I didn't have to see the magazines so accessible.

Reading and looking at those magazines has put so much trash in my mind that I believe it has robbed me of a great deal of joy and love I could have shared with my wife. It is hard to put into words, but the visual images and sexual encounters described in the magazines are still in my head and I still have to deal with that everyday, even when I hold my beautiful wife.

My recommendation to anyone wishing to get the most from marriage is—*avoid* those magazines.

DEAR MR. WILDMON:
I am a victim of pornography, having been introduced to it as a preteen through *Playboy* magazines which my father had collected and stored in his parents' upstairs closets. For a time I stayed with my grandparents and one evening came upon the magazines and sought to satisfy my natural curiosity. Little did I realize the extent of influence and emotional misery that my introduction to pornography would bring into my life.

I am a born-again Christian and was at the time, but the desires and appetites which were awakened so long ago have plagued me to this day. By the grace and help of God, I strive for purity of mind and body. . . . I will support you as I am able by prayer, sending letters and cards to [TV] sponsors and when possible with a contribution of money.

Please pray for me. I find these sexual feelings very difficult to surrender to Christ. The effects of having received and meditated on pornography at various times over a number of years lurks as a subtle deceptive enemy; for me it is the sin which so easily besets me. I find temptation almost everywhere I go in the world at large: the way women dress, or don't, in public; magazine covers and newspapers; television and movie ads in the paper. Many Christian women dress provocatively. I pour out my heart to you because I believe you are one of the very few who may understand.

I'm married [to] a lovely wife. Our sexual life is far less than satisfying for either of us. That too I am sure is directly attributable to the influence of pornography in my life. I find that my will and self-discipline have been weakened and feel I have been robbed by the Prince of Evil and by myself. God, who is ever gracious and merciful, encourages me and gives me needed grace as I yield my will to His own. I sense that many others must suffer silently as I have done, and that perhaps God will one day use me to aid them in their desire to be free of the bondage of pornography.

DEAR REV. WILDMON:

I want you to know that I am supportive of what you are doing. Public awareness has never been more needed than now.

I would like to share . . . what happened to me as a young man. It was in the mid-'60s. Art theaters were just starting to change their names to XXX, and the "stag" movie was going public.

About the same time the adult book market was also going through a change. Up to this time most magazines were still showing semiclad, suggestive pictures, but never total frontal nudity or male-female poses. That type of book was probably available, but not over the counter.

I had plenty of free time and wasn't a Christian. One day I was walking down a street and passed an empty store front. I stopped; inside was a large room with thousands of brand-new, slick-covered magazines with full frontal nudity—nothing left to the imagination.

Don, when my eye hit those pictures, something snapped in my head. It was as if a switch was being thrown. I feel I developed a "pornographic mind" through this experience.

I had never seen anything pornographic up to that time. Today, a four-year-old can see it, and they, in fact, grow up with it. How tragic.

From that day, and for several years after becoming a Christian, I have fought a battle with temptation in that area. My mind was affected, and except for the transforming power of the Holy

Spirit through Jesus Christ, I am sure I would have been driven to some deeper involvement by now.

Today, God has delivered me from a pornographic mind and I am thankful. But I fear we have many who are sick in this area with on one to share it with.

God bless you. You are in my prayers.

DEAR BROTHER:
I have a twofold purpose for writing you today. First, I am enclosing a page from the March 1985 issue of *Playboy*. It contains a letter regarding your worthy crusade. I first heard of you on our local Christian radio station via James Dobson's *Focus on the Family*. I called WATS number of the convenience store chain and politely registered my displeasure at their continued selling of pornography.

So much for my Dr. Jekyl side; now I wish to confess my Mr. Hyde side. I am opposed to pornography, but I do find that I enjoy it. I . . . have purchased only two issues of pornography in my life; but as you know, you don't have to buy it to let it get into your soul. I find myself going into secular bookstores just to look at *Playboy*, *Penthouse*, and other magazines.

I also found that when I did purchase those two magazines, that as soon as I put the magazine down, in a few minutes I would pick it back up again.

I am ashamed and guilty over this. It always leads me to sin . . . then a request to Christ for forgiveness. I have been in this cycle for over 15 years. Please pray with me that the Lord will deliver me.

DEAR MR. WILDMON:
I want to help. I was raped as a seven-year-old by my mom's boyfriend. He was always talking about *Playboy* and other magazines. Thank God, someone has finally started to care. I'm 16 years old and I've had nightmares for the past nine years. I feel his raping me was started by the ideas that the magazines put in his mind.

MR. WILDMON:

I listen to your radio broadcast every morning on the way to work, and I want to thank you for your efforts to expose the evils of pornography. I guess I relate the most to the evil that pornographic materials can have in relation to children, for I was sexually molested at age nine by two brothers, both of whom kept explicit sexual pictures hidden in their home. The Lord has since healed the emotional scars left by what happened so long ago, but I still feel very strongly for children who are the innocent victims of the twisted minds of some adults.

DEAR REV. WILDMON:

I am a former addict of pornography, and naturally I believe very strongly in what you're doing.

Before I briefly tell you about myself, I want to tell all the parents who read this to take what I'm about to say to heart and not to forget it, lest the same thing happen to their children.

I bought my first *Playboy* when I was about ten years old, simply by telling the druggist it was a birthday present for my dad, and for the next 25 years I went downhill. Over this period of time I've seen this industry grow and become more decadent every year, until the things on TV are worse than that first magazine I bought.

I hope that people will finally wake up and realize that this smut is so dangerous. I was raised in a Christian home, but eventually experimented with drugs, and started to drink and smoke, all of which I know resulted from the inroads that I had given Satan. I thank God that I never became homosexual or abused women and children, but I tried just about every other thing that was shown in pornography. The mental abuse especially at times was excruciating, to the point that I thought several times about ending the misery by taking my life. . . .

For those who don't feel threatened by [pornography], I can only say go into a hard-core bookstore and let your eyes be opened, not only to the wares being sold, but also to the individuals who frequent these places. I guarantee you it's something you'll never forget.

Pornography has been, is, and will be a threat to each and every one of us as long as we let it continue in this country.

DEAR REV. WILDMON:
I'm a pastor whose heart is breaking because of what a woman in my congregation is going through because of her husband's pornographic bookstore philosophy.

Though her husband claims to be a Christian and claims to love her, he continues to frequent a local pornographic bookstore and believes one of pornography's basic erroneous philosophies: that women need and actually enjoy being dominated and humiliated.

Through tears, she has told me her husband has a drawer full of "adult toys" along with books and magazines for inspiration. Almost daily he invades her body with one of these toys and insists she keep it within her until he gives her permission to remove it. Almost every night he spanks her bared bottom first with his hand or paddle, then with his belt. This is usually only the prelude to the "games" that follow. Through the course of the night, it is not uncommon for her to be bound and have every orifice violated. For a time he added to her humiliation by taking Polaroid pictures of her degradation.

Counseling this woman, who herself is a beautiful Christian person, has opened my eyes to the effect pornography has even on church folks.

REV. WILDMON:
I'm a junior high teacher and I see every day the effects TV, movies, and obscene magazines have on these children. They call each other [obscene names] to be funny, and make all sorts of crude remarks to teachers and other students in school.

The teachers and administrators are powerless to control it because it has gotten so out of hand. They bring obscene books, etc., to school instead of reading good literature. It's no wonder; they had the TV for a baby-sitter for years and are permitted into R- and X-rated movies, no questions asked.

The poorest families on welfare have HBO which brings R

and X material into their homes.

DEAR REV. WILDMON:

Pornography has caused me and my family much heartache, heartbreak, and pain.

As a young man of approximately 12, I was introduced to so-called "men's magazines" by a friend who got them from his father's bedroom, and we viewed them during the weekend while I stayed at his house. I started collecting *Playboy* and others then and kept them hidden under the mattress under my bed so my mother wouldn't find them. I began to develop a porno-picture imagination and imagined indulging in sexual intercourse with the women in those magazines.

I was married at 19 to a nice girl. She was three months pregnant at the time, for I had forced her into sex while petting. After we were married, I continued to experiment sexually both in marriage and in extramarital affairs. The pornographic literature continued to goad me into the "ultimate experience." Of course, that is a lie and has captured many young people. While married I seduced several women and even forced my attentions on several who threatened to tell if I did it again. These were usually friends or acquaintances of the family and went along with me to a point.

Also, I acquired another indulgence, marijuana, which is advocated in a positive manner in pornographic literature such as *Playboy*, *Penthouse*, and *Hustler*.

I even had an "affair" with our 13-year-old baby-sitter which continued for three or four years. I would show her pictures of young girls posing nude to encourage her to be more free with herself toward me.

Eventually I found that "elusive dream nymph," as depicted in all of the fantasy involving pornographic magazines, and left my wife and children to pursue the "happiness" I thought I needed and had been programmed to look for.

That soon wore off and during the occasion of traveling out of state to continue our rendezvous, I was caught in a thunderstorm in a small private plane. I prayed there and God got my attention.

Soon afterward, in July 1980, I came to myself and surrendered my life to Jesus Christ and broke off the adulterous relationship.

My wife wouldn't have me back, as she had in the meantime found out that I'd had other times of being unfaithful. She sued for divorce on grounds of adultery. Also, others gave sworn testimony to my illicit affairs. I tried to win my wife back, but there was no way. Also, I'd contracted herpes from the last girl, and my wife certainly didn't want that!

I thought of suicide, but knew the Lord had a plan for my life; and He had given me enough faith to know that that was not His will for my life.

My children (teenagers) have since found out much of the details of my former lifestyle, which has damaged our relationship. Even now, living for the Lord and serving Him these past four years has not erased the things I've done in the lives of others. I have asked the forgiveness of those I've been able to contact and all have expressed that they do forgive me. Several asked me to forgive them for their sin against me, which I did, of course.

It is certainly true: "Sow a thought, reap an action; sow an action, reap a habit; sow a habit, reap a character; sow a character, reap a destiny"—it has happened in my life. I am thankful that God has come to me to reveal my sin and has given me the opportunity to repent, believe, and receive His forgiveness through the blood of the precious Lord Jesus, my Lord and Saviour.

All of the suffering because of my reading pornography! I wish that I'd been blind—then I'd never have seen it. Even today, if I don't guard my thoughts and discipline my mind, I find myself wandering into fantasies of sexual events as they are replayed onto the fantasy-screen of my memory and imagination.

DEAR SIR:
I was watching you on the *Donahue* show and I was very relieved to find out that someone feels the way I do. This is the first time I've ever heard about people that cared about what is on TV. A long time ago I was molested (I was only 15) and this

person had *Playboy* and all kinds of pornography. I guess different children's minds work different, but mine told me that this might not have happened if he didn't have this stuff around.

I've never told anyone this because it would hurt my family, so I wouldn't want it to get around. But for a long time people around me made me feel like I was just being silly for feeling so strongly about the rotten things on cable and TV. I can't tell you how relieved I am to know that I'm not the sick one. I'll help any way I can. Just tell me what to do.

DEAR DON:
I have been molested by a very close and trusted relative. I thought this was something that always happened to girls. Not only once did this happen but many times—involving different relatives. I didn't know until I was 18 years of age that this was not a usual occurrence in households. My sister was also a victim as was my mother when she was young.

Now I am 40 years old, and I am by God's grace learning and developing a proper attitude of love and trust toward men. I lost one marriage because of wrong ideas about myself—thinking I was an "also-ran" and didn't matter. Even my second marriage was doomed to failure until Christ found me and held me and lifted me up and saved me.

What hurt the most was that in the midst of all this happening, over the years, my mother never did anything about it. She knew and still refused to do anything at all. Today Christ in His mercy has shown me that my mother . . . did all she knew how to do. She also was frightened and paralyzed by her own fears.

There were always "dirty" books and magazines around our house.

DEAR MR. WILDMON:
I attended the rally in Birmingham and was so moved by your address that I intend to get involved. I became a Christian at age 18. Before this, I had been involved in a local rock band and the drug scene. I was also very "into" magazines such as *Playboy*, etc. After becoming a Christian, I had much difficulty in over-

coming the influence of pornography and the resultant "casual sex" lifestyle to which I had become accustomed. I have since found that the seemingly innocent influences to which I had exposed myself as a youth have caused me severe problems throughout my adult life. These problems have affected my marriage, the way I relate to others, and numerous other areas. I am extremely concerned about other people making the same mistakes I have made, particularly young people.

I appreciate your work. I see you standing alone sometimes, but still standing. And as we have observed your stand, we are becoming bolder to join you and stand for the truth. I sincerely believe that, had you not listened to the call of God in these areas of concern, that many of us would be oblivious to the severity of our situation. Thank you. I know it hasn't been easy.

I finished my bachelor's degree work recently and have joined a national accounting firm to pursue my career. The Lord has blessed me in many ways, and I am ready to close the gaps and stand for His truth in my corner of the world.

DEAR DON:
I have been a victim of pornography. As an eighth-grader, I was raped. My neighbor was a man of about 19 years of age. He tied me up as a game to see if I could get loose. After I was tied up, he showed me pictures of sadomasochism, then raped me. I did not tell anyone out of fear and was raped twice more. I have lived with this secret for ten years and have only told my wife of the incident. Please remove smut from our society!

DEAR BROTHER WILDMON:
It seems that nearly everywhere I go I am tempted by porn—in stores, at work, in people's homes, even on the TV. I've been thinking about selling my TV. Maybe then I would get back into God's Word. I used to enjoy studying His Word. Pornography has destroyed that desire. Each time I give in to pornography I feel so guilty and wish I hadn't.

Pornography and a "pornographic mind," if I may use that phrase, robbed me of many blessings and my self-respect, destroyed my prayer life, and made me ineffective as a witness for the Lord.

Pornography and my sinful past recently destroyed my marriage; my wife couldn't handle it. I also am not allowed to see my children except under supervision. I can't change the past, but by the grace of God I will be delivered from this terrible sin.

Please pray for me! I greatly desire God's will in my life, but pornography has a strong hold on me! I want to be free from this sin!

DEAR BROTHER DON:

Here is a letter from my 15-year-old son who is now in a state school and addicted to pornography:

"I used to go to Dumster's anytime I got the chance to look for dirty *Playboy* books. After a while I got to the point that I had to see these books. I had to see naked women. I mean I looked at them so much that I actually wanted to rape a girl. I am serious. I still think about it even now. Lucky I'm in a state school."

DEAR SIR:

My ten-year-old niece was sexually assaulted by her stepfather who had a stack of pornographic magazines in his house. The man admits the magazines excited him.

These are the kinds of letters to which those stores that sell pornography, as well as those who defend pornography, turn a deaf ear.

11.
How Victims of Pornography Can Restructure Their Lives

Helping people overcome the damaging effects of pornography is such a new area that there is really very little material available on the subject. However, some guidelines which we follow when calling upon God to heal the hurts caused by any other sin apply in the healing process of the damage done by pornography. Knowledge of God's Word, and the forgiveness found through Christ, is central to the healing of hurts caused by all sin.

From my experience I have concluded that pornography is addictive just like alcohol and gambling. Therefore, it is best to leave it alone. Stay away from it. Nearly every person once involved with pornography with whom I have had experience says that as long as he or she can keep it out of sight and out of mind, that is the best way. In those weaker moments, find something else to give your attention to. Seek out God. Ask His leading. Each time you win that one battle, it makes it easier to win the next battle.

Pornography hurts the soul as well as the body. The body often heals far quicker than the soul. The hurt, the guilt, the memory, the humiliation—these often remain for years. There is a need for victims of pornography to feel clean in their souls, to know God's forgiveness and healing. Like any other healing, the wounds left by pornography sometimes take years to heal.

Of all the correspondence I have received from those who have been victimized by pornography, either by someone else or by being addicted to pornography, every single one said that he or she found healing and wholeness only with the help of God. If you will go back and reread the letters in the last chapter, you will notice that this is a recurring theme in them.

I once asked readers of the *NFD Journal* to share with others any expertise they had in the area of counseling the victims of pornography. Usually, we would be bombarded with letters from such a request. But because the subject was the healing from the wounds caused by pornography, the response was very small.

A Minister Offers Help

One minister did respond with what I consider some helpful material. Dr. Dennis D. Frey, a Church of the Nazarene minister of United Association of Christian Counselors, Int., certified counselor, gave the following suggestions:

As a pastor and counselor, I have been called upon to assist persons who have fallen into the trap of pornography. The problems associated with recovery are many, and few easy answers have much value. I offer the following insight in the hope that it will be of some help to you.

This . . . will deal with one limited aspect of recovery. It assumes a born-again experience on the part of the counselee and regular participation in a Christ-centered and Bible-believing church.

Grief caused by memory is a serious and primary hindrance to full recovery for the victim of pornography. The mind programs all information received and stores that information for future reference. The difficulty arises over the fact that active participation on the part of the individual is not necessary in order for the brain to retrieve stored information. Thus, the victim of past pornography abuse may suffer immense grief as a result of being bombarded with his past sin. Memory may be quite vivid, and since the individual has now ceased abusing his mind (and quite possibly his body) with illicit materials, this memory recall may well trigger a renewed desire for participation.

The individual who fails to receive competent counseling dealing with the difficulty of memory may well "give up," feeling that it is hopeless to ever be free from the desire for pornographic indulgence. Here is where the services of a capable pastor or Christian counselor are indispensable. I stress *capable* pastor and *Christian* counselor. Seeking help from a liberal pastor or a humanistic counselor may well drive the person deeper into despair.

Through proper counseling, the victim of pornography must come to understand the following truths related to the problem of memory:

1. That "a man reaps what he sows" and there will be a necessary period of time in which the person submits himself to the lordship of Christ for the purpose of restructuring. Time will vary with the individual and degree of abuse the mind has experienced.

2. That there is a great deal of difference between voluntary and involuntary recall. This difference must be dealt with in detail.

3. That the individual must be scrupulously honest in avoiding any stimulus which might trigger recall. This, of course, does not involve those "unavoidable" things which all of us must face in the course of living in a fallen world.

4. That in time memory can be *reprogrammed* in such a way that the person gains confidence over the fear of memory. This must be stressed, for it gives hope to the hopeless; however, it must be clearly understood that this reprogramming is done in partnership with the Holy Spirit as one matures in grace.

5. That time once spent in pornographic activities must be redirected and restructured so that wholesome and godly activities take the place of the time once spent in illicit activities. It is amazing how much time many persons

spend in pornographic pursuits. Unless time is properly structured, boredom may well serve as the catalyst for renewed sin.

6. Finally, the person must be taught the power of God's Word in relation to overcoming unsound memory. The correct use of selected texts, and claiming of promises can be the richest source of combating the difficult problem of involuntary recall.

Certainly this is only a "touch on" answer to the problem of grief caused by memory. But, knowing this much will give hope and relief to the victim of pornography. Following up with capable counseling in most cases is a must.

A Christian Finds Help

Another Christian wrote to tell how he is fighting to overcome addiction to pornography. He told how he struggled for years trying to stop buying, reading, and viewing pornography. He said he found some help from an organization entitled Sexaholics Anonymous. You might check to see if there is a chapter in your community. A portion of the young man's encouraging letter follows:

One day I was reading an article in a magazine about a group called Sexaholics Anonymous. The article said that the group was based on the principles of Alcoholics Anonymous and offered hope to the person who was addicted to lust. Out of desperation, I wrote to them. I was put in contact with other people in the program and began to attend meetings. I was amazed to find out that there were other people out there who had the same problem I had. Through those meetings I've started to recover from my illness. My friends, my Christian life, and the way I look at women has been transformed. I know now that I can love a girl without being sexual with her. Life is a whole new ball game.

In another situation, a young wife wrote about finding out that her husband was addicted to pornography and shared how she overcame the hurt. She had this to say:

I have been listening to your report on pornography for several years on stations KITA and KSOH, Little Rock. Until recently, this subject seemed far away from my life. May I share my story with you? I am a newlywed of approximately seven months and am married to a wonderful Christian man—a man truly given to me by God. We are both in our early twenties and dated several years before being married. I am a Christian of 13 years, my husband too. Both of us come from strong Christian backgrounds and are conservative Southern Baptists. God has blessed our marriage and both of us are truly happy in it.

Recently, while making the bed, I happened upon several magazines under the mattress. I was shocked and filled with grief when I pulled them out—*Playboy* and *Penthouse!* My dear, sweet, innocent husband could not be involved in this filth, I wanted to believe. It didn't affect people like us, or so I thought. Through my tears I looked through the magazines asking God to show me why my husband had done this. I am an attractive woman and we have a fulfilling sex life. As I glanced through the magazines, I saw such evil, felt such sinful sensations. Yes, such evil could be enticing, but, oh, how wrong. After a day of fasting and prayer, I confronted my husband in a loving way, not condemning. He confessed to me and to God with tears rolling down his face. "I have a problem. I've had it since eighth grade. It was available, so I got involved in it."

That night I watched him burn the magazines, and with a prayer give his problem over to the Lord. He has felt such release and freedom since that night. He was a Christian but Satan had a stronghold in his life. My husband is confident the problem is gone; however, we both know Satan will attack again and again. Where can we go to avoid such attacks? They're everywhere—TV, advertisements, books. I reminded myself and my husband of Jesus' priestly prayer for us in John 17, where He claimed us as His own and asked God to keep us from evil.

I can honestly say I was not angry at my husband throughout this incident—only hurt and confused. But my anger at Satan is overwhelming, my anger also at the gas station attendant who sold such magazines. Though I know God washes as white as snow, the pain is still there. I pray a hedge of protection about my husband, but what else can I do to fight this evil? For we fight not against flesh and blood, but against principalities . . . and all sorts of evil. I would appreciate any information on how I can help my husband stay pure and how I can help in this fight against pornography in the city of Little Rock.

Steps to a Cure

Notice that key steps toward overcoming a pornography problem are fasting and prayer and confession. Commitment to deal with the problem is another step (evidenced by the husband's burning of his magazines). And it was essential for him to allow God to intervene and help.

As I said earlier, the best cure for addiction to pornography is to leave it alone, to stay away from it, to find something else to do when the urge strikes you and stay involved until that urge leaves. Pray, read, find some activity to fill your time. Stay near friends and family. Just their presence will give you support and serve as a strong deterrent to giving in. Remember that each time you win one battle, it makes it easier to win the next battle.

Notice what the young wife said in the last paragraph: she wanted to know how to help in the fight against pornography. Here is another recurring theme in the letters I receive from those who have been victims of pornography—they are now fighting it. This can be a strong help, to actively join the battle to help get rid of that which has hurt you. By spending your time fighting that which destroys and hurts, you gain strength in opposing it. This could very well be a key point for those addicted to pornography. Spend your time and energy fighting it instead of letting it control you.

If your husband or wife is addicted to pornography, deal with him or her in a loving, understanding, helpful manner. This approach will help more than all the condemning you can do.

If you have been victimized by another because of pornography, forgive that person. Ask God to help you heal the wounds which the victimization brought.

More and more our society is seeing the results of pornography. In the years ahead, the church will find that helping the victims of pornography overcome their hurts will be an increasing necessity. We have allowed this sin to grow by leaps and bounds in the midst of our silence. We must not be foolish enough to think that we will not have to pay the price for our silence. We will. We will reap what we have sown.

I hope that we will not be foolish enough to follow the pattern of a purely secular answer in dealing with those victimized by pornography. Pornography affects the soul of man, and a secular society does not recognize that soul.

12.
What Can We Do?

For a few seconds Michael Juzwick just stood and looked at the open display of pornography for sale, shaking his head in anger. Then he did something. Later he explained:

"I was on my way into the La Mirada Post Office and it was like I had run into a brick wall. I thought to myself that this was government property, and I couldn't believe that the U.S. Government endorsed that type of material!"

Juzwick referred to at least seven news racks displaying pornographic newspapers just outside the post office building. The local post office personnel told him he would have to address his concern to the U.S. postmaster in Washington, D.C.

Michael did just that; he filled out a complaint card and sent it to Washington. One week later, the pornography was removed.

In a nearby city, Juzwick spotted three pornography and homosexual news racks right in front of the post office. Again, local post office personnel were no encouragement, so Juzwick went to the police. The police were of little help, so he proceeded to city hall. Michael Juzwick made his point and in a few days the pornography was gone.

Helping organize and pushing for local action campaigns in his area, Juzwick says: "There are things going on . . . that have to be dealt with, and God has called on us to do our part.

I'm talking about pornography, the decay in our homes, our lifestyles and the importance of our stewardship. I've seen too many churches stand back, afraid to get involved, afraid of the enemy, afraid to make waves. But while those people have kept to themselves, Satan and his demons have been at work. And if you don't think so, look around—at news racks and magazine stands, at what is on TV. . . . We must stand up and speak out, and then we will declare God's victory!"

A pornographic bookstore in Stoughton, Massachusetts closed its doors after a year-long battle. When the store opened in August 1982, some 3,000 townspeople drew national attention with their candlelight vigil to protest the opening.

A few days less than a year later, residents gathered again in a candlelight vigil to celebrate the closing of the store. Said one Stoughton resident, "It took 12 months and about 55,000 miles of picketing, but we fought for what we believe in and we won. I'm just elated."

Cheri Wallgren of Ashland, Illinois became concerned about the pornography in her community and decided to do something about it. She watched the video cassette "The Fight for Decency" along with about 30 members of her church. Then the members of her young adult Sunday School class spent six weeks studying the course "Christianity and Humanism." Members of her church also subscribed to the *NFD Journal.*

She said that her church was moved to action in the small town of Ashland. There were four businesses selling pornography in her community. She wrote about what happened:

"Because of your articles and the knowledge they provided, we had what we needed to approach these businessmen. After *much* prayer and 100 signatures, we presented our letters of concern, as well as several reprinted articles from the *NFD Journal.* . . . I had never done anything such as this before, but it was easy with all the support NFD gives and with the power from God." All four stores pulled the pornography.

Stories like this continue to come into our office. One person will care enough to get involved—a person who had never done anything before. And because of that person's involvement, stores pull pornographic magazines, stop selling or renting pornographic videotapes, pornographic movie houses close; and often their entire community is free of businesses selling pornography.

Everything that gets done, gets done because one person gets involved. And if one person doesn't get involved, nothing ever gets done.

Officials Praise Citizen Involvement

Little Rock Police Chief Walter E. Simpson praised a local decency group for their work in pushing their prosecuting attorney into bringing charges that forced four pornographic stores out of business. Simpson pointed out to members of the Coalition of Citizens United for Decency that "we were up against a brick wall in the judicial system until you started making noise."

At the same meeting, Pulaski County Sheriff Carroll Gravett told the group that "you can pat yourselves on the back for putting these people out of business. What we need most is public support, and that's what you have been doing."

Both the chief of police and the sheriff urged the decency group to keep the pressure on law enforcement officers, prosecutors, and judges to "make us do our jobs."

It is not enough simply to have knowledge. We must act upon that knowledge. The only reason that pornography has grown to become a multibillion dollar business, and caused immeasurable suffering, is that we have failed to act.

There is much that one person, or a small group of persons acting together, can accomplish. But nothing can be accomplished without some action.

One of the things that can be done is picketing of stores which sell pornography, either convenience, drug, or other stores selling pornography. During the past several months, several thousand stores have stopped selling pornography, including stores in the 7-Eleven chain, once, as mentioned, a chief outlet for offending magazines. Many of these stores have done so because of picketing by local citizens. Picketing is one way to help rid your community of pornography. You do not need large numbers to be successful in picketing.

How to Organize a Picket

After learning of a store that sells pornographic magazines, get a small group of leaders together and seek a meeting with the manager of the offending store. Ask politely that the pornographic magazines be removed. Explain your concern and reasons.

Should the manager refuse to quit selling the offending magazines, get other concerned individuals involved. Do not be discouraged if some area ministers or individuals you think should be concerned fail to cooperate. As few as three people can do an effective job.

Meet together at least one week prior to the selected day of picketing and ask a qualified member of your group to serve as picket captain. This individual must be the *only* person in your group authorized to speak to the media.

The picket captain should carefully study and memorize media responses such as:

● You ask why we are picketing. We want our efforts to focus attention on the proliferation of pornography in America. Many drug or food stores are noted as being "family" stores. Our picketing says that "we believe pornography does not belong in the family marketplace." Although pornography is a national problem, a major part of the solution is local.

● In picketing these stores, you are exercising two of our most basic constitutional rights: the right of free speech and the right of citizens to peaceably assemble. Both of these constitutional rights may be freely exercised but only in a nonviolent manner.

● We are saying to the seller of pornography that our community doesn't want pornography in our community. We are helping establish community standards.

Rules for Picketing

1. Arrive at the picket site 15 minutes early. Your picketing must be restricted to public property. Do not walk in the street,

and do not attempt to enter the store. No literature is to be distributed.

2. Do nothing which would interfere with a patron's right to enter the store. Do not harass any persons who enter or leave the store; do not even attempt to engage them in conversation. Do not block the entrance to the store. Leave space between yourself and your fellow picketers so that any patrons may easily enter and leave the premises.

3. Do not engage in dialogue with passing motorists. This could create a traffic hazard. Use signs approved by the group only.

4. If the owner of the premises or someone acting in his behalf asks you to leave, depart immediately without argument or confrontation. Your captain should then call the police to enforce your right to picket. Do not respond to any attempts by someone to engage you in conversation or arguments. When the police arrive, resume your picketing.

5. Should you encounter pickets or persons supporting these establishments, continue to walk in a peaceful manner but do not respond to any attempts at confrontation. If attempts are made to confront you by such persons or groups, sometimes it is best to peacefully leave the scene and your captain will call on the police to supervise the picketing.

6. Remember that you are doing a good thing. Your attitude should not be vengeful. Be pleasant to all, and especially those who oppose you.

7. You will hear that your picketing is actually helping sell pornography by drawing attention to its existence in the stores. The opposite is true. Their selling of pornography is no secret. *Do not speak to the news media, make public statements, or mention your local church name.* Refer the media to the picket captain. Again, he or she should be versed in the proper manner of response.

Additional Reason to Oppose Pornography
Here are additional statements that can be given in defense of picketing:

1. Pornography is both antifamily and anti-Christian. We are attempting to call attention to this fact and *encouraging consumers to take their business elsewhere.*

2. We believe that all people who are concerned about the welfare of our children, the rapidly rising rape rate, and the moral climate of our country should consider shopping in stores which do not sell pornographic magazines. We encourage them to boycott and urge others to boycott stores which sell pornography.

3. In exercising our basic right of free speech and the right of citizens to peaceably assemble, we hope that through the exercise of these rights we will call attention to the growing menace of pornography in our nation.

Pornography should be opposed because of several reasons. Here are a few:

1. Pornography conditions readers to deviancy. People are not born deviant. They are conditioned to it. Pornography not only causes but sustains sexual interest in deviant behavior.

2. Pornography provides malignant fantasy material which often is acted out in real life.

3. Pornography dehumanizes and debases women, makes a mockery of a beautiful gift of God, reducing sex to a cheap animal commodity to be bought and sold in the marketplace of prurience.

4. Pornography desensitizes the observer to sexual aggression against women and children.

5. Pornography presents the message that pain and humiliation are "fun" for women and cause men to be less inhibited against rape.

6. Pornogrpahy acts as a sex manual, instructing the consumer *how* to do the act.

Picket Signs
Here are ideas for possible wording for picket signs:
Stop Pornography Now
Pornography Hurts
We Want a Porn-free Community

Pornography Causes Rape
Protect Our Children—Sell No Pornography
Pornography Is Not Wanted Here
Pornography Contributes to Child Abuse
Pornography Destroys
Stamp Out Smut
Save Our Children—Stop Pornography
We Support Decency
Pornography Is a Menace to Our Community
Pornography and Crime Go Hand in Hand
Pornography Hurts Our Community

It is a good practice to keep sign wording simple and general. Nothing defamatory should be said of a store manager or of a particular store. Signs should be large enough and bold enough to be seen easily from a distance.

It is important that the community know of your concern and efforts. You should let the media know of your plans to picket. Prepare a press release and mail to the papers, radio stations, and television stations in your area. Address it to the "News Department." On your press release put the name and phone number of the local contact person at the top of the page. Mail the release not later than four days prior to your picket. Be sure to double space your release. Here is a sample press release. Reword as desired for your group.

NAME OF YOUR GROUP
PHONE NUMBER OF CONTACT PERSON

(*Name of your group*) will picket the (*name of store selling pornography*) located at (*address of local store or stores*) next Saturday, April 27, from 10 A.M. until 5 P.M. Purpose of the picketing is to draw attention to the pornography being sold at the store and to encourage concerned citizens to help rid our community of pornography by boycotting stores which traffic in pornography. While more than 20,000 U.S. stores have ceased selling pornography in the past several months, (*name of store*) refuses to stop despite being asked to do so by concerned local citizens.

A recent study made at the University of New Hampshire showed that the states with the highest readership of the anti-Christian, pornographic magazines also have the highest rate of rape. According to Dr. Victor Cline of the University of Utah, the rate of rape has gone up 700 percent since 1933, taking into account the population growth.

(*Name of your group*) has asked (*name of the store*) to cease selling pornography and (*name of the store*) has refused.

Add anything which you feel would be significant to the press release. By informing your media about the picketing, you will let your entire community know of your concern, and will pick up some support. Of course, you should be prepared to be criticized by certain voices in the media. But don't let this deter you.

How to Reply to Responses
Here are some typical responses to picketing activities as raised by people in the media. Team captains should carefully study the responses and think about what may be prompting this kind of thinking; then they should carefully digest the proper way of replying.

RESPONSE: *Pornography is really harmless as I see it. And furthermore, a Presidential Commission reported some years ago that there were no real dangers.*
A. (1) The Majority Report of the Presidential Commission on Obscenity and Pornography was called a "scientific scandal" by many in the scientific community. It was rejected by the U.S. Senate by a vote of 60 to 5. The Hill-Link Minority Report of that Commission was read into the record in both houses of Congress as a "responsible position on the issues." The Hill-Link Report cited numerous instances where evidence was suppressed when it went counter to the predetermined "findings" of the majority report. The Hill-Link Report and the chapters by Dr. Victor B. Cline in "Where Do You Draw the Line?" exposed the Majority Report for what it was. In addition, studies in the Hill-Link Report show linkages between exposure to

159

obscene material and sexual deviancy, promiscuity, affiliation with criminal groups, and more. However, extremists who want obscenity laws repealed, as the Majority Report recommended, began a campaign in early 1977 to have the report resurrected and considered a reportable document.

(2) The Supreme Court in Paris Theatre vs. Slaton (June 1973) said: "The sum of experience, including that of the past two decades, affords an ample basis for legislatures to conclude that a sensitive, key relationship of human existence, central to family life, community welfare, and the development of human personality can be debased and distorted by crass commercial exploitation of sex."

R. *You can't legislate morality.*
A. On its face, this cliché is absurd, because every law legislates morality. Every law sets some standard for its citizens, and every citizen must ultimately make the moral decision to obey or disobey. Private morals are private, public morals are the business of the entire community, and the officers empowered by the community to defend the welfare of the community against the willful minority. Commercial obscenity is public business. It is public morality that obscenity laws are designed to safeguard, not private morality.

R. *Obscenity is in the eye of the beholder. What is obscene to you may not be obscene to others.*
A. This implies that obscenity is subjective. It is not. It is the description or depiction of specific sexual activity, the description or depiction of which is prohibited by law, to protect the common good. It is as objective as stealing or murder.

R. *I'd rather see people make love than make violence.*
A. There is no love in pornography. It is totally loveless, debasing women, children, and humanity in general. In addition, violence is inherent in pornography.

R. *War, poverty, hunger, and violence are the real obscenities. Sex is not obscene.*
A. The extension of the word *obscenity* to cover all kinds of

social evils is a recent development in our language. It is a well-known technique to confuse and blunt the force of obscenity law. Of course sex is not obscene. It is the design and creation of God. It is the debasing abuse of sex that is obscene. And as in the past, so now all over the country, legislatures and the judiciary definitely specify certain abuses of sex as obscene.

R. *If you don't like pornographic films and books, you don't have to see them or buy them, but don't interfere with my right to see or buy them.*

A. I don't see or buy pornography. But it is there polluting the environment in which I am trying to raise my children. Society says it does not want it there and has enacted laws against it. It is against the law for anyone to sell or exhibit obscenity to you. We are simply encouraging the store not to sell pornography and encouraging concerned people to boycott the store as long as it continues to do so.

R. *Freedom of expression is protected by the First Amendment.*

A. It most certainly is. But the Supreme Court has said and has always held, that obscenity is not protected by the First Amendment. It is not protected expression, any more than libel or slander are. Obscenity is not a First Amendment issue. It is a crime, and most of the traffic in hard-core pornography in the country is controlled by organized crime.

R. *Who are you to tell me what I can see or read? You are imposing your morality on me.*

A. Nobody can tell you what to see or to read. But the community can tell you what commercial spectacles and literature cannot be sold or distributed to you—if you choose to live in that community. Certain drugs cannot legally be sold. The community sets up standards for itself, and has a right to legislate to protect those standards. Nobody is imposing his morality on anybody. It is only the consensus of the community that determines the standards of public decency. When that consensus is properly manifested in public law, that is community or public morality, not "ours."

R. *If pornography were allowed to flow freely, people would get bored and the problem would take care of itself.*
A. This boredom or saturation theory is invalid. Heavy users of pornography do not get bored. They go deeper and deeper into more and more bizarre forms of it. Pornography is addicting. Remember, every day children are seeing pornography for the first time. Pornography strikes at children in the mails, on newsstands, etc.

R. *The pornography industry is flourishing and growing, so the American people must want it or simply don't care.*
A. Certainly there are many who want it. That's what makes it so profitable. And obviously there are some who don't care. But all surveys show that the majority of Americans are opposed to the traffic in pornography and want it stopped. The majority do care; but they are confused and discouraged in the face of highly organized industry and the loud prophets of false freedom.

Lawyer Refutes Censorship Clichés

In Latrobe, Pennsylvania a group of citizens picketed and boycotted local stores that sell pornography. They did so because they believed they had the right to spend their money where they chose. They chose not to spend their money in stores that sell magazines which promote child abuse, rape, and incest.

An editorial in a Pennsylvania newspaper referred to the boycotting citizens as "vigilantes" who were crusading for censorship. An attorney, Craig Roth, quickly responded with a letter to the editor. "I have concluded," wrote Roth, "that the social cost to our children and families caused by our local pornography is unacceptably high."

Here, from the newspaper, is Roth's eloquent reply:

The First Amendment guarantees freedom of the press. This right includes the freedom to publish and distribute publications without prior submission to federal, state, or local government censorship or licensing. This provision has absolutely *no* application to the actions of private citizens. It is only a restraint on governmental power and authority.

When citizens speak out against pornography, they are exercising their fundamental and cherished right of free speech. This freedom also includes association with other likeminded people for the advancement of ideas and beliefs. This is guaranteed by the same First Amendment that protects freedom of the press. Free speech is not limited to trivial topics. Exercise of free speech for the advancement of ideas on important public topics is never censorship. Put the "censorship" label back on the shelf.

In addition to this, the Supreme Court has repeatedly ruled that obscenity is not within the area of constitutionally protected speech or press. In fact, it is a criminal offense to produce, distribute, or sell obscene material.

[The editorial writer] referred to those people attempting to have pornography removed from our community as "vigilantes." A vigilante is a person who takes the law into his own hands. Again, *no* application can be made to people lawfully exercising their fundamental rights of speech and association on important public issues.

It is time to put away the phony labels and face the issue at hand. Several other misconceptions need to be addressed:

MYTH: *Citizens cannot advocate removal of pornography because morality is involved and people cannot agree on what is moral.*

FACT: Moral judgments are routinely made by almost all citizens and government officials every day on many issues. Moral judgments are made whenever laws are enacted forbidding rape, theft, fraud, defamation, child abuse, etc. Moral arguments of child safety are used to support the need for a new middle school. Everyone makes moral judgments, pro or con, on pornography. Why can't they be expressed with equal validity as on any other topic?

MYTH: *We dare not prohibit the publication of the outstanding interviews and stories published in pornographic magazines.*

FACT: If this printed material is as outstanding as suggested, the authors should have no problem publishing in alternative publications.

MYTH: *Local pornography is sold only to adults, so juveniles never see it.*

FACT: True, pornography, like beer, is sold only to adults. But who would argue that juveniles do not illegally consume beer in Williams County? The same is true of pornography. Just a few weeks in our juvenile court would quickly dispel the notion that juveniles lack access to pornography.

MYTH: *Today, it's repression of pornography; tomorrow, it's essays on government, religion, etc.*

FACT: This worry is only legitimate in the area of governmental censorship or licensing. Private citizens lack the authority to censor anything. All people can do is exercise their fundamental right of free speech and association to advance their common beliefs and ideas. The "today it is pornography but tomorrow it's serious literature" argument is a worn out cliché. Applying the cliché by analogy may lead one to refuse to allow the garbage collectors to pick up bags at curbside because tomorrow they may pick up the patio furniture behind the house.

MYTH: *Popular pornography such as* Playboy, Penthouse, *etc., has no deleterious effect on our community.*

FACT: Some of our local child sex abuse cases involve offenders with significant usage of soft-core pornography.

In one local case of father-daughter incest that began at age 5, the teenage daughter said her father read (not saw) of various oral sexual acts and techniques in *Playboy* and then performed the acts on her.

In the recent case of the school psychologist, *Playboy* magazines were discovered in his home, along with hard-core pornography.

In two recent cases of male pedophiles molesting teenage boys, large quantities of *Playboy, Penthouse, Hustler,* and X-rated videos, such as are available locally, were used as lures in the seduction and entrapment of their male victims.

These "harmless" magazines promote and encourage sex with children. Sex between children and Santa Claus has been a favorite Christmas topic of *Playboy* and *Penthouse. Penthouse* has featured pictorials in which adults are made to look like children. *Playboy* and *Penthouse* have used cartoons that promote child sex abuse.

Both proponents and opponents of pornography can cite studies that have been done. Basically, science is incapable of telling us with certainty what injury pornography does to our community. But then, science has never demonstrated much proficiency in the realm of human values. Are we left without any guidance? I believe the answers lie in the good common sense of our people.

Over 110 sexual abuse cases have been investigated over the past two years and three months in Williams County. Our silence regarding pornography is partly to blame for our current problem. How long can our community continue to absorb the cost of destroyed children and families?

Picketers Talk

Recently a friend of mine told me about going into a store which had a large sign which read: *"We do not sell pornography."* The store was located near another store which was being picketed because it sold pornography. When my friend asked the owner why the sign, he replied: "Those picketers are really hurting the business of those who sell pornography, and I don't want them coming in here and picketing me." So you see, picketing of stores selling pornography does help.

Most of us are reluctant to picket because of the past history of many who have abused and misused this freedom. However, once we have overcome this reluctance, picketing takes on a different perspective.

Mary Kay Esswein of Cypress, California wrote me of the effects of the picketing she organized against 7-Eleven stores in her community prior to 7-Eleven's recent decision to stop selling pornographic magazines. Her letter:

I am excited about the "ripple effect" of the 7-Eleven picket in early August. In our area it has sparked Christian citizens to speak out against pornography in the following ways:

● Lake Cable Commission, planning to carry the Playboy Channel, had 60 citizens protest at public hearing.

● Los Alamitos City Council is considering an ordinance to control "sexually explicit" materials in news racks.

● Long Beach City Council is considering an ordinance

165

to place "sexually explicit materials" in another room when video games are present.

● Many letters to the editor of Long Beach *Press Telegram*.

● For this reason, I see great potential of the next picket as well, to bring decency to our country. Praise God! The battle is rugged and the process is slow, but "greater is He that is in us, than he that is in the world."

We were surprised at the supportive waves, honks, "bless you's," and "hang in there" by passing motorists. Several concerned citizens stopped to ask how they could help.

Others have written similar responses. Darleen Burbart of Plattsmouth, Nebraska wrote: "What a wonderful feeling to know that you have opposed the devil on the front lines. If there is a need for another picket, we will give it everything we've got including recruiting people from our church and other churches. This has awakened our church. Thank you for the opportunity you gave us to have the courage of our convictions."

Donald E. Logue, a St. Petersburg pastor, wrote: "Here in our church, several people agreed to picket who had never done that before."

"If there is another picket, please advise us as soon as possible. Most people were very supportive of our efforts," wrote Barbara Morgan of Maywood, Illinois.

Michael A. DeRoss of East Haven, Connecticut said: "The experience was one I'll never forget, and I look forward to doing something of this nature again."

"What do you think the possibility would be to do this on a monthly basis? Several people in our church made this comment," wrote the Rev. Bob Caviness of Arlington, Texas.

"We here in Columbus, Georgia had a tremendous time of spiritual blessing doing the picketing," wrote Christina Ellyson of Fort Benning, Georgia.

Carolyn DeLong of Beaver Crossing, Nebraska wrote: "It was a great day picketing the 7-Eleven stores."

Rick Shonkwiler of Cincinnati shared the feeling a year or so ago. "Keep the pressure on 7-Eleven. Thanks for calling the picket. I believe the message got out. We had three or four people join our picket when we explained what we were doing."

Karen L. Randolph of Belleville, Michigan wrote some months ago: "One 7-Eleven manager risked his job by taking the trashy literature off his shelves, and he wants us to continue to picket so he can be backed in his decision."

Ron Shuping of Belmont, North Carolina wrote: "Thank you! I've never picketed in my life and if it hadn't been for the NFD, I never would have had the determination to not only get involved, but also enlist others. Saturday was a victory."

The Rev. Bob Jones of Sugar Land, Texas wrote: "We, along with members of several churches, picketed, and the results were truly praiseworthy!"

Scott Lee Frey of Bethlehem, Pennsylvania wrote: "Thanks so much for calling this to our attention and helping us to get a picket organized. We've waited so long for someone to say, 'Here's how to do it!' "

"Dear Manager" Cards

Another thing you can do is to have printed several "Dear Manager" cards and distribute them to stores selling pornography in your community. You can encourage your church and other local churches to get their members involved in distributing the cards. Leave the *"Dear Manager"* card with the manager of a family store in your community that sells pornography. Tell him or her of your concern about the effects of pornography. Follow up your complaint with a letter to the owner of the store.

On one side of the cards you could have printed some general information such as this:

Revealing Statistics
● 1977   One million teen-age girls—one out of every ten—get pregnant each year . . . sharpest increase in those under 14 (*Newsweek,* Sept. 1, 1980).
● 1978   16.3 percent of all live births were illegitimate

(*Statistical Abstract of the U.S.*, 1980, p. 660.)
● 1982   20 million Americans now have genital herpes (incurable venereal disease) (*Time*, August 2, 1982).

On the other side, have this or a similar message to the manager printed:

Dear Manager:
I came into your business and noticed that you sell pornographic magazines. I believe that pornography does not belong in the family marketplace. As long as you continue to sell these magazines, I cannot in good conscience shop in your store. I am taking my business elsewhere and encouraging my friends not to shop here. I hope you will reconsider and stop releasing this type of anti-Christian, antifamily material on our community. If you should decide to stop selling pornography, please call me at the number listed below. I will at that time resume shopping in your store and will encourage my friends to do the same.
Signed_____
Phone Number_____

Give this card to the store manager when you enter a store that sells pornographic magazines.

Other Things You Can Do
There are several other things you can do either as an individual or in cooperation with a group or members of your local church.
1. Immediately begin a massive education program informing members on the situation and calling them to involvement. This could be done through Sunday School material and/or other organized studies.
2. Call together the leaders in the community and churches to discuss the situation, give information, and educate them on the seriousness of the situation, and begin a plan of action.
3. Ask for the strong enforcement of existing laws and, where needed, passage of new laws to deal with the situation.

4. Encourage an expression of Christian stewardship by selective buying (boycotting stores selling pornography).

5. Encourage members to write to elected officials asking for strong enforcement of obscenity laws.

6. Ask store managers in the area to discontinue sales of pornographic magazines. Urge local church members to boycott those stores in the community that sell pornographic magazines. Educate and enlist others in the battle.

Rules for Success

In your efforts, there are some things you should always remember:

1. Do not be overly concerned with numbers. You can start with one, or two, or three people. You can be much more effective with a few committed people than with hundreds of lukewarm supporters. Remember the victory of Gideon. Much can be accomplished as we realize that the Lord says it is "not by might, nor by power, but by My Spirit."

2. Do not be discouraged when individuals who should be concerned criticize or make light of your efforts. Many of these simply have no knowledge of the problem. If you should question them, you would often find glaring ignorance on the issues. Enemies can turn up in some strange places. But it comes with the territory.

3. Keep the whole process simple at first. If you have only a few people, do one project at a time, and do it simply. Do not attempt to put a complex organization together at first. You may want to begin simply as a letter-writing group. Or you may want to get people together and picket a pornography outlet.

4. Organize. You need to bring together others who are concerned into some type of group. This gives substance and identity to your efforts. One person cannot do it alone. You must have organization, and responsibility must be shared. To successfully accomplish your goals responsibility must be shared. Try to get the right people involved. Your efforts can be quite effective in gaining the exposure needed to increase the size of your group.

5. Meet regularly—as often as possible. The most successful groups meet regularly for prayer, fellowship, and planning.

6. Get informed. Begin by informing yourself concerning local problems of obscenity, pornography, and indecency. If cable television is available, become familiar with all that is being released on your community via cable. Visit drug stores, convenience stores, etc., to determine the prevalence of pornography in your community. Read the *NFD Journal* each month. If you do not receive the *NFD Journal,* write NFD, P.O. Drawer 2440, Tupelo, MS 38803. We will send you a complimentary copy of the *Journal.* You can then subscribe and begin getting much needed information each month.

7. Write the President. Ask the President to issue an order to the attorney general ordering vigorous prosecution of federal obscenity laws. The address: President of the United States, The White House, Washington, D.C. 20500.

8. Write letters to the editor of your local newspaper concerning issues of decency. This is a good way to help establish community standards.

What Pastors and Other Leaders Can Do

If you are a pastor, Sunday School teacher, or leader in your church, you can help in other ways. For example:

1. Address the issues of indecency, pornography, and obscenity in a message on a regular basis.

2. Examine offerings on cable TV from regular fare to HBO, Cinemax, Showtime, etc. Make these matters of prayer and preaching.

3. Learn what the Playboy Channel is about. If you have cable, your area either already has the Playboy Channel, or it is on the way.

4. Write denominational leaders asking, "What are we doing as a denomination to address these issues?"

What You Can Do in Your Church

If you are simply a member of your local church, you can do the following:

1. Find out where your pastor stands in the battle against obscenity, pornography, and indecency. Pray for and support your pastor in the education of other members of your church. Share with your pastor any helpful information you find on the issues.

2. Share information with members of your Bible study group, Sunday School class, etc.

3. Get other members to join you in the "Dear Manager" card campaign and/or picketing, etc.

4. Write denominational leaders and ask, "What are we doing to address the problems of indecency, pornography, and obscenity?"

Recommended Reading
To help you become informed, I recommend that you obtain copies and read carefully the following publications:

Francis Schaeffer, *A Christian Manifesto* (Westchester, Illinois; Crossway Books, 1981).

John Whitehead, *The Second American Revolution* (Elgin, Illinois: David C. Cook Publishing Company, 1982).

Franky Schaeffer, *A Time For Anger* (Westchester, Illinois: Crossway Books, 1982).

Christianity and Humanism: A Study in Contrasts: Published by NFD—Six-week study for church, Sunday Schools, etc. Available from NFD office, P.O. Drawer 2440, Tupelo, MS 38803.

James Hitchcock, *What Is Secular Humanism?* (Ann Arbor, Michigan: Servant Books, 1982).

Humanist Manifestos I and II (New York: Prometheus Books, 1973).—Stated beliefs of humanists.

How to Fight the Playboy Channel
I urge you to begin working to keep cable pornography out of your community now, even if it isn't currently in your communi-

ty. The Playboy Channel is making attempts to market its pornographic TV channel in various markets across the country. You can help prohibit the Playboy Channel from bringing pornographic TV into your community. But your chances of being successful are infinitely greater if you will fight it before it arrives, not after! It is much easier to stop the Playboy Channel on the front end—before it comes to local cable.

Many people think that because they don't subscribe to cable, they don't have to worry about pornography. Let me share with you the following letter from a pastor in Mexia, Texas:

Dear Don:
I enjoy your paper. I feel that we as Christians need to stand up and be heard. Your work is helping us to be aware and take that stand.

I was recently made aware of a shocking fact that I was totally ignorant of. I am a minister and father of three pre-teen children—two girls and a boy. My wife and I keep a close eye on the programs our children watch. We are using an antenna to receive our signal because of the problems of cable viewing.

I was at home enjoying a quiet evening relaxing. Our children were in bed, and I had finished watching the evening news. Instead of turning the set off and going to bed as usual, I thought I would see what was on. I turned through the channels and watched a few minutes of each program instead of checking the channel guide as I generally do. I came across our local adult channel (VUEW) which is "scrambled" so you cannot receive the signal. I was shocked to find that the channel was not as scrambled as I had thought. The picture was very plain at times, and not completely scrambled at other times. The sound could be heard with no problem at all. The show was nothing but an XXX movie at its worst. I watched a 30-minute program between the time of 11 and 11:30, a time when during the summer months our children are very likely to be awake. During that short time period several different couples were totally nude. There was no problem at all with making out the full nudity and sexual acts they were performing. There were at least two of those scenes involving group sex. The language was straight from the gutter of sin.

Thinking this to be just one of those nights when the signal was just affected by the weather or whatever, I spot-checked this so-called scrambled channel for the next two weeks. I always found the same thing. I also found that the best picture came in during the sexual acts and faded during the other parts.

If I were on cable I would say, "Take it out," but I am on an antenna and the only thing I can do to get this trash out of my home is to get the set out. Please advise us, if you can, as to what can be done to remove VUEW from the air-waves of our country.

Television pornography isn't always found only on cable; often it on the regular channels.

What can one do? Step one is to get together a select group of Christian leaders to address the issue. Show this group actual videotapes taken from the Playboy Channel. We can provide you with a copy from the NFD office if the request is made on your letterhead. These films dispel the Playboy marketing myth that the channel is "sophisticated adult entertainment." The films demonstrate that the Playboy Channel is not about naked ladies or erotic adventures. It is about sexual perversion. That will be clear once the tapes start rolling. Playboy for the most part has taken X-rated movies, slightly edited, and developed its service from these. There is nothing remotely "adult" or "sophisticated" about it.

The group should choose representatives (get organized with the best leaders available) from among themselves to serve as a steering committee for the entire group. This group should meet every week for prayer and strategy.

The next step is for the group to go to the local cable franchise and seek removal of the Playboy Channel, or to show the local cable system the Playboy tape and secure a commitment from the cable system not to carry the channel in your community.

If the cable franchise is uncooperative, then the group should plan a mass meeting in which a larger group of community Christian leaders participate. All community ministers, business, and civic leaders should be invited. Again, the videotapes should be shown. The problem defies description. The tapes are the only means for showing the depth of the problem. Get members from the first group to invite others to come to the larger meeting. At this meeting explore any ports of entry supporters may have with members of the city council. Decide who would best serve as spokesman to the city council. Plan for effective community participation in the battle.

Members at the second meeting should set a date to go en masse to a city council meeting to present their concerns. At this meeting, tapes from the Playboy Channel should be shown to the council *prior to* the discussion. Then the council will properly understand the concern.

Then the group should discuss with the council the destructive nature of the pornographic channel and let it be known that community standards are violated by the Playboy pornography service. The local council can refuse to grant a cable franchise to the company if the cable company refuses to stop airing the Playboy Channel or decides to air the channel. However, don't be discouraged if the council members refuse to get involved. Remember, elected officials are often more *politician* than *statesman*.

Pastors should then schedule a Sunday for addressing the issue from the pulpits and encourage congregations to express objections to the cable franchise. Postcards could be passed out during the Sunday morning worship for members to sign and send to the cable franchise. The card could read as follows:

Dear Manager:
It has come to my attention that (*local franchise*) is making (or planning to make) the pornographic Playboy Channel available in our community. I object to the Playboy Channel which features heterosexual and homosexual sex scenes

in depraved detail, group sex, and other sexual perversions. I know that such material will ultimately be viewed by many of the children in our community both accidentally and intentionally. Believing that sex is a beautiful gift of God to be enjoyed in marriage, I object to _____'s decision to carry this type of anti-Christian, antifamily programming. I respectfully request that _____ reconsider its decision and drop the Playboy Channel from the cable system.

Signed _____

Phone Number _____

The group should issue local press releases to call attention to the movement. Many people who are with you in principle will become involved once you gain their attention.

If the group decides it is in their best interest, a major community-wide decency rally could be held at a central, neutral site. The organization I head, the National Federation for Decency, would be happy to assist as needed in plans for the rally.

When all other avenues have been explored to no avail, and the local cable system continues to carry Playboy, then the group should call for a cancellation Sunday. This would be a Sunday when ministers would again address the problem from pulpits and call for members to fill out an order to cancel their cable service. Very often this is the only effective way to rid the system of the blight of Playboy. The cancellation form can be distributed to each member of the congregation during the service. Cancellation notices should be distributed during the worship service after the pastor has preached on the subject and need for involvement and commitment. People should be asked to sign the cancellation notice *while in the service*. Take up the cancellation notices before the benediction. These can then be combined from all churches and turned in to the cable company at one time. The cancellation notice is a legal document. If the cable company refuses to disconnect the service (as they often do), the subscriber should refuse to pay any future bills. Be sure the cancellation notice is in three parts—one for the household canceling, one for the local cable company, and one for the group sponsoring the drive.

If the Playboy Channel has not yet arrived in your community, your task is simpler. As mentioned it is much easier to deal with the problem before it arrives.

Letters from Crusaders
Thousands of concerned people are now involved in fighting pornography. Here are sample letters:

> **Dear Don:**
> Recently a group of concerned Christians in our small community viewed your video, "The Fight for Decency." Everyone was moved to subscribe to the *NFD Journal* and to consider what we might do to rid our community of the sale of *Playboy* magazines from our local drugstore. One concerned woman sent a kind and thought-provoking letter to the owner of the drugstore, who lived a hundred miles away. He was not even aware that the magazine distributors had placed them in his stores. He responded positively, expressing his concern for decency by not only pulling the pornographic material from our community, but from the five other stores he owns throughout western South Dakota. One letter from a concerned Christian, a caring drugstore owner, the encouragement from NFD, and decency has taken a giant step forward in and beyond our community. Thanks for your work and dedication. We have learned what one person can do!
> ——Concerned Christians for McLaughlin, S.D.
> *(One person who tries can accomplish more than one million people who never try. God wants people who try.)*

> **Dear Mr. Wildmon:**
> Just wanted to write a note to say that I privately approached the owner of a food store here in my small town,

and without hesitation he agreed to *discontinue* his pornographic magazines. You can imagine how exhilarated I was and am. He has the only substantial food business in town, and as far as I know he was the only one selling pornography.

I cannot help wondering how many others across the U.S. would do the same if they were approached privately in a spirit of humility. I feel as though a door remains open for me to share Christ with this man now. What a sad thing for the Lord's sake it would have been had I picketed his store *first*. He would have resented it and rightfully so. I feel as though the Bible teaches that public pressure should be applied *only* when private means have been exhausted. If we have approached offenders with a spirit of meekness and shown respect, then they have no ground of complaint if it becomes necessary to apply public pressure.

Thank you for your work and efforts. You have motivated me to take action. By the way, I have followed up my visit with the owner by sending him a letter thanking him for his concern and courage.

Mr. Wildmon:
I am happy to report that the town of Collierville is now without any outlets for pornographic magazines or X-rated rentals. In December 1984 there were five such outlets and with the NFD and Porno Plague as guidelines for dealing with this matter, all material has now been removed from the dealers' shelves.

Our goal now is to continue to get a sufficient law that will prevent any outlet, including the Playboy Channel, from establishing a means to bring this back to our community.

Dear Rev. Wildmon:
I want to thank you for sending Bethany a subscription of the *NFD Journal*. Every time a new issue comes to me, I pick out some company that is relevant to my situation in

life, and I write. Enclosed you will find a copy of a letter I wrote today.

I want you to know that until I got your magazine, and started listening to Dr. James Dobson's *Focus on the Family*, I felt that battling the moral decay of our society was a hopeless effort. This frustrated me constantly. It has been the *NFD Journal* that has given me hope and confidence, especially the reports of success you give. I have even seen results in my own small community, where, over the last year I have seen pornography pulled from three stores.

Mr. Wildmon:
I have now become courageous enough to courteously tell a shop owner that I will no longer buy at his store, but will come back when the pornography is gone. Before I received the encouragement of the *NFD Journal*, I thought such an expression of rebuke was fruitless. Now I know from your reports, and have seen from my own experience, that it really works.

The information from the *NFD Journal* also gives me the facts that I can assimilate in order to communicate to my members, and give them the same confidence that you have given me.

May God bless your efforts as you have blessed mine.

13.
How to Start a Local Antipornography Group

During the past few years I have learned the importance of being organized. So much more can be accomplished when people work with and through an organized group. That is the reason we began local chapters of the National Federation for Decency. The material in this chapter will help you begin a local group. It is written toward starting a local chapter of the NFD, but can be adapted to begin an independent local group. However, our experience has shown that being part of a national organization that can provide help allows the local group to be stronger and the national organization to be stronger.

The National Federation for Decency is a citizen's organization promoting the biblical ethic of decency and Christian values in the American society. Anyone desiring to start a local chapter should contact the National Federation for Decency, Post Office Drawer 2440, Tupelo, MS 38803.

NFD's Relationship to Local Chapters

1. Provides current information on matters pertaining to decency. Many people remain unaware of the negative impact of sweeping changes which have taken place in network and cable television, and in the availability of pornography in the family marketplace. NFD focuses attention on these and other matters

related to decency and Christian values through widespread contact with religious leaders, pastors, community leaders, and concerned individuals nationwide.

2. Encourages affirmative economic action for decency. NFD supports and encourages citizens in the use of economic expression to bring about decency. NFD has found that a most effective way to combat pornography in the family marketplace is by refusing to purchase products from outlets selling pornography and by encouraging friends to do likewise.

How to Get Started

1. Start yourself as a committee of one! If you desire to start a local group in your community, first contact the NFD and let us know so we can help. Then begin by *informing yourself* concerning local conditions. You can start in your living room. Examine television for content and values presented. What is it teaching? If cable is available in your area, familiarize yourself with *all* that is offered through your local service.

To discover the prevalence of pornography, visit the drugstores, the bookstores, the local movie houses, convenience markets, etc. Pornography is all too easy to recognize. *Know what you are up against in your community.*

2. Involve others. Form a group of likeminded people who have expressed a sincere desire to become involved. Keep the *organizing* group small. Attempt to attract opinion leaders in your community, individuals who know how to get things done. Try to get people from a variety of religious backgrounds. Be certain that your members are respected members of the community, preferably family men and women. Avoid fanatics. Avoid strong political affiliations. Balance is extremely important. You will be more effective as an organization if you represent a good cross-section of the community.

3. Get organized. Set a date, time, and place to have a meeting. Attempt to find a central location. Suggested procedures at first meeting include: introducing everyone, explaining the need for a chapter and purpose of your first meeting, explaining the *importance of being organized,* describing methods by

which your goals can be accomplished.

The methods will include, among others, the following:

(1) *Letter writing.* This will be one of the primary strategies of the group. Write letters to TV stations and advertisers, letters to editors, and letters to pastors and community leaders urging involvement. These could be done at the actual meeting. Responses could be shared at subsequent meetings.

(2) *Organizing special projects.* Each *NFD Journal* will list areas of concern and suggested action.

(3) *Distributing literature.* Much is available through NFD headquarters.

(4) *Contacting people.* Remember: our work is primarily educational, and most people simply have not been given all the facts on vital issues relating to decency in our communities and our nation.

(5) *Recruiting new members.*

(6) *Addressing local needs.* Other methods and opportunities will become apparent to you as your chapter grows.

Appoint a nominating committee to study the most qualified members for various offices. Set place, date, and time of the next meeting. The nominating committee should make recommendations for at least three committees:

The Public Education Committee should write letters to advertisers, newspaper editors, newspaper publishers, judges, pastors, city councils, district attorneys, businesses. The committee provides speakers where they can be used.

The Legal Assistance Committee advises the chapter in various matters. It acts as a liaison between the chapter and the judicial.

The Financial Development Committee has the job of raising funds for your chapter operations.

It is most important, in all your activities and meetings, to maintain a Christian attitude. Open and close your meetings and gatherings with prayer. Dedicate your chapter organization and work to the glory of God. Remember that you are taking the Christian approach to countering those forces which would destroy Christian values. Remember the words of Paul: "I can do all things through Christ who strengthens me" (Phil. 4:13).

The Importance of Being Organized

• First, an organization provides a highly desirable and efficient means of gathering and distributing information and materials to its various members. Most people, as individuals, do not have the necessary time and money to subscribe to, and read, all the periodicals, newsletters, books, and circulars that would be needed to keep them well informed.

By having an organization with a research staff, however, a participant can have quick and reliable access to a wide range of materials that the staff obtains, reads, analyzes, condenses, and then makes available to the members, together with desirable and recommended courses of action. The National Federation for Decency will serve local groups in this capacity.

• Second, organizational machinery provides for cohesiveness and unity of action by the entire group. This is important in two factors: nature and timing. By "nature" we mean what the members do. They work on the same things. They have one goal or a series of goals. They do not waste and lose individual strengths by attacking everything in general and nothing in particular. One hundred members organized and disciplined toward one goal will accomplish far more than a thousand members inspired but disorganized.

By "timing" we mean that even organizational efforts need to be expressed in a definite time. Timing is extremely important for one to exert influence to the greatest degree. The strongest of men will accomplish nothing by throwing a punch after his opponent has retreated. A million people opposing a piece of legislation, even if they are organized, will accomplish virtually nothing if they wait until the legislation is approved before expressing their opposition. By having the organization well informed and disciplined, its power can be timed and exerted just at those prime moments when the greatest influence can be exerted, and the greatest hope of victory enjoyed.

● Third, organizational influence, as opposed to many indvidual ones, provides a tremendous economy of time. This applies, as we have noted, in the gathering of materials. It applies in the distribution of materials; it applies even more importantly in mobilizing the group for action. If telephones are chosen for the means of communication, an entire organization can be informed on a course of action literally within minutes, and can begin action. How haphazard and time-consuming, on the other hand, would be the task of trying to get an unorganized group of people to the same level of information and action!

● Fourth, organization provides for tremendous clout and influence. There are several sound reasons for this. For one thing, in an organization that is well integrated and harmonious, the leaders of the group can speak confidently of representing the views of dozens, hundreds, or thousands of members, as the case may be. The individual or office being addressed knows that the speaker is relaying the views of all the members, just as though they were there in person.

In summary, a person can hope to accomplish far more with his own personal views and influence if these are expressed as a part of an organized group with the same views.

Chapter Membership or Association

Though any honest, sincere person dedicated to NFD-type efforts can or could be a chapter member, persons in certain work or positions should be sought and encouraged to participate. The idea is to have the talent, experience, and willing hands to operate a balanced and effective chapter. In every area there are these folks with these attributes who do and don't know of NFD work or of your efforts in it. So your publicity will get some and your recruiting will get others.

To establish your Christian ethical base, recruit pastors, church lay leaders, and other influential Christians. Include people from the legal, medical, and law enforcement areas; enlist social workers, media and community leaders, local government officials, public educators.

Recommended Structure for Chapters

Though any chapter may be originated by one or two persons who are interested in NFD work, seek to build a strong organization which will accomplish your purpose. It is better to have persons on your board(s) who are really interested in this work rather than ones with "big names" who aren't.

Start with: president, secretary, treasurer. These see to the beginning and early tasks and work of interested people. The positions of president or equivalent, secretary, and treasurer should remain functional as the focal point of the chapter. Relationship between president and board(s) would be established as best suits each chapter.

Build to a comparatively small executive board whose function is to make plans and give guidance. A larger group, commonly called the Board of Governors, should also be organized. These are people in a position to recruit help in making the chapter's projects successful. It is a big plus to have several pastors on the Board of Governors.

Bylaws should be prepared by your chapter.

Comments, Pointers, and Miscellaneous

1. Talk with and meet with interested people before organizing.
2. Talk with pastors, educators, etc., and pass out NFD material.
3. Get coverage for your activities from local TV and radio stations and newspapers, especially those that are Christian in emphasis.
4. If you fail to get good response from a church's leadership, work through an interested member.
5. Remember that some secular media and businesses are sympathetic with certain of NFD's goals, especially in the area of pornography.
6. Members of executive and governing boards should pledge or secure funds for chapter operations.
7. Every chapter should involve as many concerned citizens as possible.

As we have stated earlier, you can't do everything, but you can do something. What you can do, by the grace of God *do*. And the time to get started is *now*—while you can still make a difference.

14.
A Model Obscenity Statute for Use in Your Community, City, or State

One of the most effective organizations dealing with pornography from the legal perspective is Citizens for Decency Through Law. CDL can give your group or elected officials expert help in the fight against pornography, and in most cases their services are free. CDL spent years developing the model obscenity law which follows. The "obscenity statute" is intended as a *model*. Before it is adopted, it will, in all likelihood, need to be modified to avoid potential conflict with particular state constitutional or statutory constraints. As a matter of United States Constitutional law, however, it is correct in its present form. If questions arise concerning the model statute, you should contact CDL. The address is: Legal Department, Citizens for Decency Through Law, Inc. P.O. Box CDL, Phoenix, AZ 85261. The phone number is 602/483-8787.

Model Obscenity Statute

An act to create and enact chapter _____ of the _____ Code, relating to definitions, pandering of obscenity, wholesale pandering of obscenity, promoting or wholesale promoting of a sexual device, making obscene drawings, disseminating matter harmful to minors, unlawful exhibition or display of harmful materials to minors, unlawful exhibition of harmful performances at outdoor theaters, deception to obtain matter harmful to minors, compelling acceptance of objectionable materials, commercial nudity, sexual exploitation of children, presumption and evidence of knowledge, injunctive actions, jury instructions concerning evidence of pandering, and legislative purpose and severability.

BE IT ENACTED BY THE CITY OR STATE OF

Chapter _____ of the _____ Code is hereby created and enacted to read as follows:

SECTION 1: *Definitions*. As used in this chapter, unless the context clearly indicates otherwise:
  (a) "Community" when used in connection with "contempo-

rary community standards," means the geographical area within the jurisdiction of the court or vicinage of the jury hearing the case, whichever is larger.

(b) "Harmful to minors" includes any material or performance, whether through pictures, photographs, drawings, writings, cartoons, recordings, telephonic transmissions, films, videotapes or other such medium, which shall be "harmful to minors" if the following apply:

(1) The average person, applying contemporary community standards, would find that the material or performance, taken as a whole, appeals to the prurient interest of minors in sex.

(2) The material or performance depicts or describes sexually explicit nudity, sexual conduct, sadomasochistic sexual abuse or lewd exhibition of the genitals, in a way which is patently offensive to prevailing standards in the adult community with respect to what is suitable for minors.

(3) The material or performance, taken as a whole, lacks serious literary, artistic, political, or scientific value for minors.

(c) "Knowledge of character" means having general knowledge or reason to know, or a belief or ground for belief which warrants further inspection or inquiry, of the nature and character of the material or performance involved. A person has such knowledge when he or she knows or is aware that the material or performance contains, depicts, or describes sexually explicit nudity, sexual conduct, sadomasochistic sexual abuse or lewd exhibition of the genitals, whichever is applicable, whether or not such person has precise knowledge of the specific contents thereof. Such knowledge may be proven by direct or circumstantial evidence, or both.

(d) "Material" means any book, magazine, newspaper, advertisement, pamphlet, poster, print, picture, figure, image, drawing, description, motion picture film, phonographic record or recording tape, videotape, or other tangible thing capable of producing or reproducing an image, picture, sound, or sensation through sight, sound, or touch.

(e) "Minor" means any person under the age of 18 years.

(f) "Obscene" means any material or performance, whether through pictures, photographs, drawings, writing, cartoons, recordings, films, videotapes, telephonic transmissions, or other medium is "obscene" if the following apply:

(1) The average person, applying contemporary adult community standards, would find that the material or performance taken, as a whole, appeals to the prurient interest.

(2) The material or performance depicts or describes, in a patently offensive way, sexual conduct, sadomasochistic sexual abuse, or lewd exhibition of the genitals.

(3) The material or performance, taken as a whole, lacks serious literary, artistic, political, or scientific value.

(g) "Performance" means any motion picture, film, videotape, played record, phonograph or tape, broadcast, preview, trailer, play, show, skit, dance, or other exhibition performed or presented to or before an audience of one or more, or transmission by means of electrical, radio, television, telephone, or other communicative device or facility to a known closed or open circuit audience of one or more or to the general public.

(h) "Person" means any individual, corporation, cooperative, company, partnership, firm, association, joint venture, business, establishment, organization, or other legal entity of any kind.

(i) "Promote" means to manufacture, issue, sell, give, provide, advertise, produce, reproduce, lend, mail, deliver, transfer, transmit, publish, distribute, circulate, disseminate, present, display, exhibit, advertise, or to offer or agree, or possess with intent, to do any of the foregoing.

(j) "Prurient" means a lascivious, unhealthy, degrading, shameful, or morbid, interest in sexual conduct, sexually explicit nudity, sadomasochistic sexual abuse, or lewd exhibition of the genitals. Materials or performances may be deemed to appeal to the prurient interest when they have a tendency to excite lascivious thoughts or desires or when they are designed, marketed, promoted, or disseminated to cater or appeal to such an interest. Where the material or performance is designed for and primarily disseminated or promoted to a clearly defined deviant sexual group, rather than the public at large, the prurient-appeal requirement is satisfied if the dominant theme of the material or performance, taken as a whole, appeals to the prurient interest in sex of the members of that intended and probable recipient group.

(k) "Sadomasochistic sexual abuse" means actual or simulated flagellation, rape, torture, or other physical or sexual abuse, by or upon a person who is nude or partially denuded, or the condition of being fettered, bound, or otherwise physically restrained, for the actual or simulated purpose of sexual gratification or abuse or represented in the context of a sexual relationship.

(l) "Sexual conduct" means ultimate sexual acts, normal or perverted, actual or simulated, involving a person or persons, or a person or persons and an animal, including acts of masturbation, sexual intercourse, fellatio, cunnilingus, analingus, or physical contact with a person's nude or partially denuded genitals, pubic area, perineum, anal region, or, if such person be female, a breast.

(m) "Sexual device" means any artificial human penis, vagina, or anus, or other device primarily designed, promoted, or marketed to physically stimulate or manipulate the human genitals, pubic area, perineum, or anal area, including dildoes, penisators, vibrators, vibrillators, penis rings, and erection enlargement or prolonging creams, jellies, or other such chemicals or preparations.

(n) "Sexually explicit nudity" means the sexually oriented and explicit showing, by any means, including but not limited to, close-up views, poses, or depictions in such position or manner as to present or expose such areas to prominent, focal, or obvious viewing attention, of any of the following: post-pubertal, fully or partially developed, human female breast with less than a fully opaque covering of any portion thereof below the top of the areola; the depiction of covered human male genitals in a discernible turgid state; or lewd exhibition of the human genitals, pubic area, perineum, buttocks, or anal region, with less than a fully opaque covering.

(o) "Visibly displayed" means that the material or performance is visible on a billboard, viewing screen, marquee, newsstand, display rack, window, show case, display case, or other similar display area that is visible from any part of the premises where a minor is or may be allowed, permitted, or invited, as part of the general public or otherwise, or that is visible from a public street, sidewalk, park, alley, residence, playground, school, or other place to which a minor, as part of the general public or otherwise, has unrestrained and reasonably anticipated access and presence.

(p) "Wholesale promote" means to promote for purpose of resale.

SECTION 2. *Pandering obscenity.*

(a) No person, with knowledge of the character of the material or performance involved, shall do any of the following:

(1) Create, photograph, produce, reproduce, or publish any obscene material, when the offender knows that such material is to be commercially or publicly promoted or when reckless in that regard.

(2) Exhibit or advertise for promotion or promote any obscene material.

(3) Create, photograph, tape, direct, produce, or reproduce an obscene performance, when the offender knows that it is to be commercially or publicly promoted or when reckless in that regard.

(4) Advertise an obscene performance for presentation, or promote or participate in promoting an obscene performance, when such performance is presented publicly, or when admission is charged, or when presented or to be presented before an audience of one or more.

(5) Possess or control any obscene material with the purpose to violate this section.

(6) Participate in the acting or posing for any obscene material or performance, or portion thereof which is obscene, when the offender knows that it is to be commercially or publicly promoted or when reckless in that regard.

(b) It is an affirmative defense to a charge under this section that the material or performance involved was disseminated or promoted for a bona fide medical, psychological, legislative, judicial, or law enforcement purpose, by or to a physician, psychologist, legislator, judge, prosecutor, law enforcement officer, or other person having such a bona fide interest in such material or performance.

(c) A person who violates this section is guilty of pandering obscenity, a class _____ misdemeanor. If the offender has previously been convicted of a violation of this section or of Section 6 relating to disseminating matters harmful to minors, then pandering obscenity is a class _____ felony.

SECTION 3. *Wholesale pandering obscenity.*

(a) No person, with knowledge of the character of the material involved, shall wholesale promote any obscene material or to offer or agree, or possess with intent, to wholesale promote any obscene material.

(b) It is an affirmative defense to a charge under this section that the material or performance involved was wholesale promoted for a bona fide medical, psychological, legislative, judicial, or law enforcement purpose, by or to a physician, psychologist, legislator, judge, prosecutor, or law enforcement officer.

(c) A person who violates this section is guilty of wholesale pandering obscenity, a class _____ felony. If the offender has previously been convicted of a violation of this section, then wholesale pandering obscenity is a class _____ felony.

SECTION 4. *Promoting or wholesale promoting a sexual device.*

(a) No person, with knowledge that the device involved is a "sexual device," shall do either of the following:

(1) Promote, or to offer or agree, or possess with intent to promote, any sexual device.

(2) Wholesale promote, or to offer or agree, or possess with intent, to wholesale promote, any sexual device.

(b) It is an affirmative defense to a charge under this section that the sexual device was promoted or wholesale promoted for a bona fide medical, psychological, legislative, judicial, or law enforcement purpose by or to a physician, psychologist, legislator, judge, prosecutor, or law enforcement officer.

(c) A person who violates this section is guilty of promoting or wholesale promoting a sexual device. A person violating subdivision (1) of subsection (a) of this section is guilty of a class _____ misdemeanor. If the offender has previously been convicted of a violation of subdivision (1) of subsection (a) of this section, promoting a sexual device is a class _____ felony. Violation of subdivision (2) of subsection (a) is a class _____ felony. If the offender has previously been convicted of a violation of subdivision (2) of section (a) of this section, wholesale promoting a sexual device is a class _____ felony.

SECTION 5. *Making obscene drawings.*

(a) No person shall make, draw, color, paint, scratch, cut, or otherwise produce any obscene drawing, writing, graffiti, picture, or other material in public or on a public place, including a public or private building, billboard, utility pole, wall, sidewalk, roadway, or poster.

(b) A person who violates this section shall be guilty of making an obscene drawing, a class _____ misdemeanor.

SECTION 6. *Disseminating matter harmful to minors.*

(a) No person, with knowledge of its character, shall promote or otherwise furnish or present to a minor any material or performance which is obscene or harmful to minors, or possess or control any such materials with the purpose or intent to violate this section.

(b) The following are affirmative defenses to a charge under this section, involving material or a performance which is harmful to minors but not obscene:

(1) The minor exhibited to the defendant or his agent or employee a draft card, driver's license, birth certificate, marriage license, or other governmental or educational document purporting to show that such minor was 18 years of age or

over and the person to whom such document was exhibited did not otherwise have reasonable cause to believe that such minor was under the age of 18 and did not rely solely upon the oral allegations or representations of the minor as to his or her age.

(2) At the time the material or performance was promoted or otherwise furnished or presented to the minor involved, a parent or lawful guardian of such minor, with knowledge of its character, accompanied the minor or consented to the material or performance being promoted or otherwise furnished or presented to the minor:

(c) The following are affirmative defenses to a charge under this section, involving material or a performance which is obscene or harmful to minors:

(1) The defendant is the parent, lawful guardian, or spouse of the minor involved.

(2) The material or performance was promoted or otherwise furnished or presented to the minor for a bona fide medical, psychological, judicial or law enforcement purpose by a physician, psychologist, judge, prosecutor, or law enforcement officer.

(d) A person who violates this section is guilty of disseminating harmful material to minors. If the material or performance involved is harmful to minors but not obscene, violation of this section is a class _____ misdemeanor. If the material or performance involved is obscene, violation of this section is a class _____ felony.

SECTION 7. *Unlawful exhibition or display of harmful materials to minors.*

(a) No person, having custody, control, or supervision of any business or commercial establishment or premises, with knowledge of the character of the material involved, shall do any of the following:

(1) Visibly display, exhibit, or otherwise expose to view in that part of the premises where a minor is or may be allowed, permitted, or invited as part of the general public or other-

wise, all or any part of any book, magazine, newspaper, or other form of material which is harmful to minors.

(2) Visibly display, exhibit, or otherwise expose to view all or any part of such material which is harmful to minors in any business or commercial establishment where minors, as part of the general public or otherwise, are, or will probably be, exposed to view all or any part of such material from any public or private place.

(3) Hire, employ, or otherwise place, supervise, control, or allow in any business or commercial establishment or other place, any minor under circumstances which would cause, lead, or allow such minor to engage in the business or activity of promoting or otherwise handling such material which is harmful to minors, either to or for adults or minors.

(b) The following are affirmative defenses to a charge under this section:

(1) The minor exhibited to the defendant or his agent or employee a draft card, driver's license, birth certificate, marriage license, or other governmental or educational document purporting to show that such minor was 18 years of age or over, and the person to whom such document was exhibited did not otherwise have reasonable cause to believe that such minor was under the age of 18 and did not rely solely upon the oral allegations or representations of the minor as to his or her age or as to the knowing consent of the minor's parent or lawful guardian.

(2) At the time the material was visibly displayed or otherwise furnished or presented to the minor involved, a parent or lawful guardian of such minor, with knowledge of its character, accompanied the minor or consented to the material being visibly displayed or otherwise furnished or presented to the minor.

(3) The defendant is the parent, lawful guardian, or spouse of the minor involved.

(c) A person who violates subdivisions (1) or (2) of this subsection (a) of this section is guilty of displaying harmful materials to minors, a class _____ misdemeanor. If the offender has previously been convicted of a violation of either of these subdivisions, then such offense is a class _____ misdemeanor. Whoever violates subdivision (3) of subsection (a) of this section is guilty of unlawfully employing a minor, a class _____ misdemeanor.

SECTION 8. *Unlawful exhibition of harmful performances at outdoor theaters.*

(a) No person, having custody, control, or supervision of any outdoor or drive-in motion picture theater or arena, with knowledge of the character of the performance involved, shall knowingly present or participate in presenting the exhibition of a performance which is harmful to minors upon any outdoor or drive-in motion picture theater or arena screen, when such screen is visible from a public highway or street, sidewalk, park, alley, residence, playground, school, or other such place to which minors, as part of the general public or otherwise, have unrestrained and reasonably anticipated access and presence.

(b) A person who violates this section is guilty of exhibiting a harmful performance at an outdoor theater, a class _____ misdemeanor. If the offender has previously been convicted of a violation of this section, then such offense is a class _____ misdemeanor.

SECTION 9. *Deception to obtain matter harmful to minors.*

(a) No person, for the purpose of enabling a minor to obtain any material or gain admission to any performance which is obscene or harmful to minors, shall do either of the following:

(1) Falsely represent that he or she is the parent, guardian, or spouse of such minor.

(2) Furnish such minor with any identification or document purporting to show that such minor is 18 years of age or over.

(b) No minor, for the purpose of obtaining any material or gaining admission to any performance which is harmful to minors, shall do either of the following:

(1) Falsely represent that he or she is 18 years of age or over.

(2) Exhibit any identification or document purporting to

show that he or she is 18 years of age or over.

(c) A person who violates this section is guilty of deception to obtain matter harmful to minors, a class ———— misdemeanor.

SECTION 10. *Compelling acceptance of objectionable materials.*

(a) No person, as a condition to the sale or delivery of any material or goods of any kind, shall, over the objection of the purchaser or consignee, require the purchaser or consignee to accept any other material reasonably believed to be obscene or which if furnished or presented to a minor would be harmful to minors.

(b) A person who violates this section is guilty of compelling acceptance of objectionable materials, a class ———— misdemeanor.

SECTION 11. *Commercial nudity.*

(a) In any establishment or premises where alcoholic beverages are dispensed, no person shall knowingly provide service without a fully opaque cloth covering of the human male or female genitals, pubic hair, buttocks, anal region, or post-pubertal female breast below the top of the areola, where such person is exposed to the view of the public, patrons, guests, invitees, or customers.

(b) No person, being the owner, lessor, lessee, or having control, custody, or supervision of any commercial business, establishment, tavern, store, shop, massage parlor, or other place of public accomodation, commerce, or amusement, shall recklessly use or promote the use of, or permit or tolerate others to use or promote the use of, such premises in violation of subsection (a) of this section, or, if given or having actual notice of such violation, shall negligently fail or refuse to cease or stop such violation, or to cause an agent, employee, or other subordinate to cease or stop such violation, or to notify a law enforcement agency of such violation.

(c) "Provide service" means the provision or allowance of services, advertisement, or entertainment to the public, patrons, guests, invitees, or customers, including hostessing, bartending, food or beverage serving or preparing, table setting or clearing, waitering or waitressing, singing, dancing, massaging, counseling, and also including beauty or figure contests, modeling, or exhibitions.

(d) It is an affirmative defense to a charge under this section if any full or partial nudity has serious literary, artistic, political, or scientific value.

(e) A person who violates subsection (a) of this section is guilty of commercial nudity, a class _____ misdemeanor. Whoever violates subsection (b) of this section is guilty of promoting commercial nudity, a class _____ felony. If the offender has previously been convicted of a violation of this section, then the degree of offense shall be one degree higher than that above provided for the particular subsection involved.

SECTION 12. *Sexual exploitation of children.*

(a) No person, with knowledge of the character of the material or performance involved, shall employ, consent to, authorize, direct or otherwise induce or allow a minor to engage or participate in the production, filming, photographing, acting, posing, or other manner of making any material or performance, when the minor will or does engage or participate in sexually explicit nudity, sexual conduct, or sadomasochistic sexual abuse.

(b) No person, with knowledge of the character of the material or performance involved, shall promote or wholesale promote any material or performance which includes, depicts, represents, or contains a minor engaged or participating in the acting, posing, or otherwise the subject of sexually explicit nudity, sexual conduct, or sadomasochistic sexual abuse.

(c) No person, with knowledge of the character of the material or performance involved, shall promote or wholesale promote any obscene material or performance which includes, depicts, represents, or contains a minor engaged or participating in the acting, posing, or otherwise being the subject of sexually explicit nudity, sexual conduct, or sadomasochistic sexual abuse.

(d) It is an affirmative defense to a charge under subsection

(a) that the minor exhibited to the defendant, prior to engaging or participating in the material or performance, a draft card, driver's license, birth certificate, or other governmental or educational document purporting to show that such minor was 18 years of age or over and the defendant did not otherwise have reasonable cause to believe or suspect that such minor was under the age of 18 and did not rely solely upon the oral allegations or representations of the minor as to his or her age.

(e) It is an affirmative defense to a charge under subsections (b) and (c) of this section that the defendant, in good faith, had a reasonable factual basis to conclude that the subject of the sexually explicit nudity, sexual conduct, or sadomasochistic sexual abuse was not a minor but was in fact over the age of 18 years.

(f) In any prosecution or action under this section, the court or jury, as trier of fact, shall make the determination of whether the subject of the sexually explicit nudity, sexual conduct or sadomasochistic sexual abuse is, beyond a reasonable doubt, a minor, and the following methods of proof shall be competent for the admission of direct or circumstantial evidence on this issue:

(1) Personal inspection or testimony of the minor or alleged minor.

(2) Testimony of the parent, lawful guardian, teacher, or other personal acquaintance of the minor or alleged minor.

(3) Inspection of the material or performance involved.

(4) Testimony of a witness to the production, filming, photographing, acting, posing, or other manner of making the material or performance involved or testimony of a physician, scientist, or other expert witness as to the age or appearance of the minor or alleged minor.

(5) Any other method authorized by law or by the rules of evidence.

(g) The subject of the sexual exploitation is presumed to be a minor if he or she is portrayed, advertised, marketed, cast, represented, or otherwise promoted or appears as being a minor.

(h) A person who violates subsection (a) of this section is guilty of sexual exploitation of a minor, a class _____ felony.

A person who violates subsection (b) of this section is guilty of pandering the sexual exploitation of a minor, a class _____ misdemeanor. A person who violates subsection (c) of this section is guilty of pandering obscenity involving the sexual exploitation of a minor, a class _____ felony. If the offender has previously been convicted of a violation of this section, then the degree of the offense shall be one higher than that above provided for the particular subsection involved.

SECTION 13. *Presumption and evidence of knowledge.*

(a) An owner or manager, or his agent or employee, of a bookstore, newsstand, theater, distributing firm, warehouse, or other commercial establishment engaged in promoting materials or performances or distributing or handling materials for promotion or wholesale promotion, may be presumed to have knowledge of the character of the material or performance involved if he or she has actual or constructive notice of the nature of such material or performance, whether or not he or she has precise knowledge of its contents.

(b) In any prosecution or action in which knowledge of the character of material or a performance or knowledge that a device is a "sexual device," is at issue, it is evidence of such knowledge that actual notice of the nature of the material was previously provided. Without limitation on the manner in which such notice may be given, actual notice of the character of material or a performance may be given in writing by the state's attorney, city attorney, or similar prosecuting authority of the jurisdiction in which the person to whom the notice is directed does business. Such notice, regardless of the manner in which it is given, shall identify the sender, identify the material or performance, state whether it is obscene or harmful to minors, and bear the date of such notice. Such notice shall also give a brief description of the contents of the material or performance and indicate whether the material or performance contains sexually explicit nudity, sexual conduct, sadomasochistic sexual abuse, or lewd exhibition of the genitals or is a "sexual device."

(c) In any prosecution or action in which knowledge of the

character of material or a performance or knowledge that a device is a "sexual device," is at issue, evidence of any of the following is relevant proof of such knowledge:

(1) The sexually explicit nature and character of the material or performance involved is advertised, marketed, or otherwise publicly exploited for the purpose of attracting patrons or purchasers.

(2) The bookstore, newsstand, theater, distributor, firm, warehouse, or establishment is advertised, held out, or otherwise represented as possessing sexually explicit materials for promotion or wholesale promotion or as promoting or wholesale promoting a sexually explicit performance.

(3) The bookstore, newsstand, theater, distributor, firm, warehouse, or establishment is primarily engaged in promoting or wholesale promoting sexually explicit materials or sexually explicit performances.

(d) In any prosecution or action under this chapter, knowledge of the character of the material or performance involved may be proven by direct or circumstantial evidence, or both.

SECTION 14. *Injunctive actions.*

(a) When there is reason to believe that any person is violating, is about to violate, or is possessing any material with intent to violate any of the provisions of this chapter, the attorney general, state's attorney, the city attorney, or prosecutor for a city may institute and maintain an action for preliminary and permanent injunctive relief, to enjoin the violation in an appropriate court having equitable jurisdiction. No bond shall be required of the official bringing the action and the official and the political subdivision shall not be liable for costs or damages, other than court costs, by reason of the injunctive orders not being granted or where judgment is entered in favor of the defendant by the trial or an appellate court. A citizen of the county may also bring such an action, but shall post a bond in an amount not less than $500. Such actions shall be brought in the name of the state.

(b) The court shall hold the hearing on the preliminary injunction within two days, not counting Saturdays, Sundays, or legal holidays, after service of the complaint and motion for preliminary injunction upon the defendants. The court shall then issue an order granting or denying the preliminary injunction within 24 hours after the conclusion of the hearing, regarding the material or performance adjudged obscene or harmful to minors. No right of jury trial shall attach to the hearing on a preliminary injunction, but the duty rests on the plaintiff to prove by clear and convincing evidence that the offense is being or is about to be committed. If the defendants who have been served fail to appear at said hearing, then a preliminary injunction shall be issued on the date of the hearing. The finding of the court regarding the obscenity or that the subject matter is harmful to minors at the preliminary injunction stage shall not be binding upon the final order on the merits at trial on the permanent injunction. The court shall reserve the right to reconsider its preliminary finding based upon any further evidence or testimony which may be introduced at such trial. If the court enters a final order denying a permanent injunction on the basis that the material or performance is not obscene or harmful to minors as a whole, then no contempt shall be found for violation of the preliminary injunction relating thereto.

(c) The court shall set the matter for a hearing on the permanent injunction according to the provisions of the rules or other order of court. The defendant shall have the right to demand a hearing on the permanent injunction within ten days of the issue or denial of the preliminary injunction. Either party shall have the right of trial by jury on the issue of the obscenity or harmful to minors nature of the material or performance involved at the hearing for the permanent injunction, and such jury shall render a special and separate verdict as to the nature of the subject matter. The duty rests on the plaintiff to prove by clear and convincing evidence that the offense is being or is about to be committed by the defendants. It shall be the duty of the trier of fact to determine all issues of fact concerning the obscene or harmful to minors nature of the subject matter, including the elements of appeal to prurient interest, community standards, patent offensiveness and serious value, without the need for expert testimony or other evidence other than the material or performance itself. Expert testimony or other evidence on these issues may be entered by either party and will be entitled to such weight as the trier of fact deems appropriate under the circumstances. The court shall then issue an order granting or denying the permanent injunction within five days after the conclusion of the trial, regarding the material or performance adjudged obscene or harmful to minors.

(d) In the event that the court issues a permanent injunction, it shall also issue an order directing a law enforcement officer to seize and hold all copies of the subject matter which are in the possession of the defendants. Such material shall be held until the exhaustion of all appellate remedies and may then be disposed of by order of the court.

(3) Violation of a preliminary or permanent injunction shall be punishable as contempt of court.

SECTION 15. *Jury Instructions—evidence of pandering.*
The following instruction may be read to the jury in a criminal prosecution or civil action under this chapter:

"In determining the question of whether the allegedly obscene material or performance involved, when taken as a whole, lacks serious literary, artistic, political, or scientific value, the jury may consider the circumstances of promotion, advertisement, or editorial intent and particularly whether such circumstances indicate that the material or performance was being commercially exploited for the sake of its prurient appeal and whether any serious value claimed was, under the circumstances, a pretense or reality.

"Such evidence is probative with respect to the nature of the material or performance and if the jury concludes that the sole emphasis was on the sexually provocative aspect, this can justify the conclusion that the material or performance is lacking in serious literary, artistic, political, or scientific value.

"The weight, if any, to which such evidence is entitled is a matter for the jury to determine."

SECTION 16. *Legislative purpose and severability.*

(a) Nothing in this chapter shall be presumed to invalidate, supersede, repeal, prevent, or preempt any ordinance or resolution of any county or city covering the subject matter of this chapter. Cities or counties may adopt ordinances and resolutions which are consistent with this chapter and must employ the language of this chapter, as written or judicially construed, for all offenses which are covered by this chapter. Cities and counties further retain the right to regulate and define offenses, locations, or requirements regarding any activities, displays, exhibitions, or materials, whether by zoning, licensing, or criminal laws, not specifically regulated by this chapter.

(b) If any provision of this chapter, including any part, phrase, or word of any section, or the application thereof, to any person or circumstance is held invalid, such invalidity shall not affect other provisions or applications of this chapter which can be given effect without the invalid provision or application, and to this end, the provisions of this chapter are declared to be severable. It is the purpose of this chapter to comply with constitutional and police power limitations, and this chapter shall be interpreted and construed to adopt or change in compliance with controlling court decisions.